RISE OF THE MACHINES

THE DYN ATTACK WAS JUST A PRACTICE RUN

JAMES SCOTT (SENIOR FELLOW – INSTITUTE FOR CRITICAL INFRASTRUCTURE TECHNOLOGY)

DREW SPANIEL (RESEARCHER – INSTITUTE FOR CRITICAL INFRASTRUCTURE TECHNOLOGY)

ICIT | Institute for Critical Infrastructure Technology

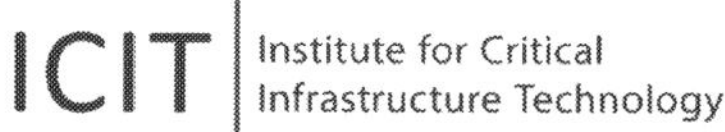

Institute for Critical Infrastructure Technology
The Cybersecurity Think Tank™
www.icitech.org

ISBN-13: 978-1-540894-57-1

CONTENTS

ABOUT ICIT: THE CYBERSECURITY THINK TANK

The Institute for Critical Infrastructure Technology (ICIT), a non-partisan cybersecurity think tank, is cultivating a cybersecurity renaissance for our critical infrastructure communities. ICIT bridges the gap between the legislative community, federal agencies and the private sector through a powerful platform of cutting edge research, initiatives and educational programs. Through objective research and advisory, ICIT facilitates the exchange of ideas and provides a forum for its members to engage in the open, non-partisan discourse needed to effectively support and protect our nation against its adversaries.

www.icitech.org

Security-by-design is an indispensable prerequisite to the establishment of vital critical infrastructure resiliency. Each device vulnerable to adversarial compromise, inflates and bolsters the exploitable cyber-attack surface that can be leveraged against targets, and every enslaved device grants adversaries carte blanche access that can be utilized to parasitically entwine malware into organizational networks and IoT microcosms, and that can be leveraged to amplify the impact and harm inflicted on targeted end-users, organizations, and government entities

—James Scott, Sr. Fellow, ICIT

INTRODUCTION

The perfect storm is brewing that will pummel our Nation's public and private critical infrastructures with wave upon wave of devastating cyberattacks. The Mirai malware offers malicious cyber actors an asymmetric quantum leap in capability; not because of sophistication or any innovative DDoS code, rather it offers a powerful development platform that can be optimized and customized according to the desired outcome of a layered attack by an unsophisticated adversary. Right now, script kiddies and cyber-criminal gangs are already drastically expanding their control over vulnerable IoT devices, which are enslaved to malicious purposes and can be contracted in DDoS-for-Hire services by a virtually unlimited number of actors for use in an infinite variation of layered attack methods.

The brunt of the vulnerabilities on the Internet and in Internet-of-Things devices, rest with DNS, ISPs, and IoT device manufacturers who negligently avoid incorporating security-by-design into their systems because they have not yet been economically incentivized and they instead choose to pass the risk and the impact onto unsuspecting end-users. As a result, IoT botnets continue to grow and evolve. Deep Web DDoS-for-Hire services increase in their availability to rent or barter for, in their profitability, and in their accessibility; thereby compounding the pandemic of havoc that will continue to be unleashed on the global IoT macrocosm.

As the adversarial landscape of nation state and mercenary APTs, hacktivists, cyber-criminal gangs, script kiddies, cyber caliphate actors, and hail-mary threat actors continues to hyper- evolve, America's treasure troves of public and private data, IP, and critical infrastructure continues to be pilfered, annihilated, and disrupted, while an organizational culture of 'Participation Trophy Winners" managed by tech neophyte executives continue to lose one battle after the next.

In late 2016, a series of high-profile Distributed Denial of Service (DDoS) attacks launched from Internet of Things (IoT) devices that were infected with the Mirai botnet set new precedents for the magnitude and impact of IoT DDoS attacks. In only a few weeks, Mirai has enabled unsophisticated adversaries to stifle free speech on the open internet, to deliver more than 1.1 Tbps of traffic to the French ISP, OVH, to overwhelm Dyn's DNS systems in the Eastern United States, to hinder heat distribution to citizens in Finland, to launch politically motivated attacks, and to disrupt the online operations of five major Russian banks. In their Q3 "State of the Internet" report, Akamai noted a 71% increase in the number of DDoS attacks from Q3 2015, a 77% increase in Layer 3 and 4 attacks, and a 138% increase in DDoS attacks that generated greater than 100 Gbps of traffic [1].

The Mirai botnet has forced stakeholders to recognize the lack of security by design and the prevalence of vulnerabilities inherent in the foundational design of the Internet of Things devices leveraged in the attack; nevertheless, Mirai will not forever remain the favorite tool of unsophisticated malicious threat actors. In fact, due to a saturated pool of bot victims, script kiddies have already begun adapting the malware to new victim hosts or adopting new malware altogether. Mirai presents an interesting case study because its operation and activity inform the security community of threat actor trends in targeting, services, and capabilities. However, rather than focus holistically on a single transient threat, Mirai, stakeholders can prevent future incidents by addressing the lack of security-by-design in the

Internet-of-Things and in the Internet itself before a script kiddie or a more sophisticated adversary employs an evolved DDoS botnet to inflict a serious impact on target critical infrastructure systems, such as Financial assets, Healthcare networks, or Energy properties.

1 | A SIMPLIFICATION OF THE INTERNET

The Internet is a network of networks in which user clients send traffic through transfer media (copper wire, fiber optics, satellite, etc.) through an Internet Service Provider (ISP) network into a Domain Name Server (DNS) provider. That traffic is then delivered to either another user client or to the server of Content Delivery Network (CDN) that caches pages of popular websites on local servers. DNS converts easy to remember website names into IP addresses and vice- versa. CDNs host servers all over the globe and they sell the ability for websites to store their heavy bandwidth content on those servers that are closest to users. Organizations rely on CDNs to store and distribute content so that their websites are not overwhelmed by too much user traffic. Despite being vulnerable targets to significant DDoS attacks, such as the Mirai incidents detailed below, CDNs and some DNS and ISPs offer website and user services that beneficially filter traffic or that absorb and redistribute abundant floods of malicious traffic; these services are marketed as anti-DDoS or DDoS mitigation services. Some private sector companies only market this service.

2 | PROTOCOLS

When data travels over a network, such as the Internet, it is independent of the medium (copper wire, satellite, etc.) on which it travels because we have defined protocols that are separate from the means of communication. Protocols are high-level abstractions of network communications that ignore how the data travels. How data travels is determined by the software and hardware at either end of the communication. Networks are built according to layered communication architecture known as a protocol stack. Each layer in the stack acts as a language for communicating information relevant to that layer. The two primary protocol stacks are the Open Systems Interconnection (OSI) and the Transmission Control Protocol and Internet Protocol (TCP/IP) architecture. When an attacker conducts a denial of service attack, they flood a target with traffic that is sent and interpreted according to the layers of these models.

ISO OSI

The International Standards Organization (ISO) Open Systems Interconnection (OSI) model details the layers at which network communications occur. The OSI model is a conceptualization of the layered activities necessary in a communication.

Table 1: OSI Protocol Layers			
Layer	Name	Activity	Protocols
7	Application	User-level data	FTP, HTTP, POP3, & SMTP
6	Presentation	Standardized data appearance, blocking, or compression	Compression & Encryption Protocols (i.e. SSL)
5	Session	Session/logical connections within an application, message sequencing and recovery	Authentication Protocols
4	Transport	Flow control, priority assignment, end-to-end error detection and correction	TCP & UDP
3	Network	Blocking message data into uniform sized packets, routing	IP, ICMP, ARP, & RIP
2	Data Link	Reliable data delivery over physical medium; transmission error recovery, packet separation into uniform sized frames	802.3 & 802.5
1	Physical	Communication across physical media; individual bit transmission	100Base-T & 1000 Base-X

The layers each add its own activity to a communication, like an assembly line. Each layer passes data along three directions. Data is communicated abstractly with the above layer, data is communicated parallel or across the same layer in another host, and data is communicated less abstractly with the layer below. Interactions with the above and below layers are actual interactions while interactions with parallel layers (peers) are virtual communications. For a sender and receiver, peer-to-peer correspondence occurs between like layers. The logical message transmission path operates from layer 7 to layer 1 for a sender and from layer 1 to layer 7 for a receiver. Physical communication always occurs across a medium at layer 1. In this way, each layer performs the same activity for a sender and receiver, just in reverse order. For instance, if the sender's layer 4 affixes a header to a message that designates the sender, receiver, and relevant sequence information, then the receiver's layer 4 reads the header and removes it after verification that the receiver is the intended recipient [2].

What layer an adversary leverages in a denial of service attack depends upon what type of traffic is employed and how the traffic is generated. Application traffic is a layer 7 DDoS, while routers network actual traffic at layer 4, and packet floods occur at layer 3 [2]. Layer 7 attacks, like HTTP/HTTPS attacks, are most difficult to mitigate because they mimic normal user behavior. A sophisticated Layer 7 attack may target specific areas of a website, making it even more difficult to separate from normal traffic [3].

TCP/IP

The OSI model has too much overhead for megabit-per-second (or greater) communications. Consequently, the Transmission Control Protocol/ Internet Protocol (TCP/IP) stack was invented to manage the Internet. TCP/IP is conceptualized in four layers, but it is defined by protocols. Despite its name, TCP/IP actually contains three protocols: TCP, IP, and UDP (User Datagram Protocol). The Transport layer receives messages of variable lengths from the Application layer and then it parses them into units of manageable size, transferred in packets. The Internet layer transfers packets as datagrams to different physical connections, based on the destination of the data. The physical layer consists of the drivers and devices that perform the actual bit-by-bit data transfer [2].

The TCP protocol ensures the correct sequencing of packets and the integrity of the data within the packets. The protocol also calls for the retransmitting of missing packets and for fresh copies of damaged packets. The TCP service can build up overhead as computational resources are expended to record and check sequence numbers, to verify the integrity of data, and to request and wait for the retransmission of faulty or missing packets. TCP packets include a sequence number, an acknowledgment number for connecting packets, flags, and source and destination port numbers. UDP lacks the error-checking and correcting features of TCP. In most DDoS attacks adversaries flood the victim system with malformed, unrequested, or recursive TCP, UDP, or ICMP traffic [2].

Table 2: Internet Communication Layers and Services

Layer	Layer Characteristics		Layer Services	
	Action	**Responsibilities**	**TCP Protocols**	**UDP Protocols**
Application	Prepare messages from user interactions	Addressing, user interaction	SMTP, HTTP, FTP, Telnet, etc.	SNMP, Syslog, Time, etc.
Transport	Convert messages to packets	Sequencing, integrity, error correction	TCP	UDP
Internet	Convert packets to diagrams	Routing, flow control	IP	IP
Physical	Transmit diagrams as individual bits	Data communication	Data Communication	Data Communication

ANATOMY OF A DISTRIBUTED DENIAL OF SERVICE ATTACK

CONSTRUCTING A BOTNET

Figure 1: Sale of a Deep Web Sale of a "Botnet Guide" for Script Kiddies

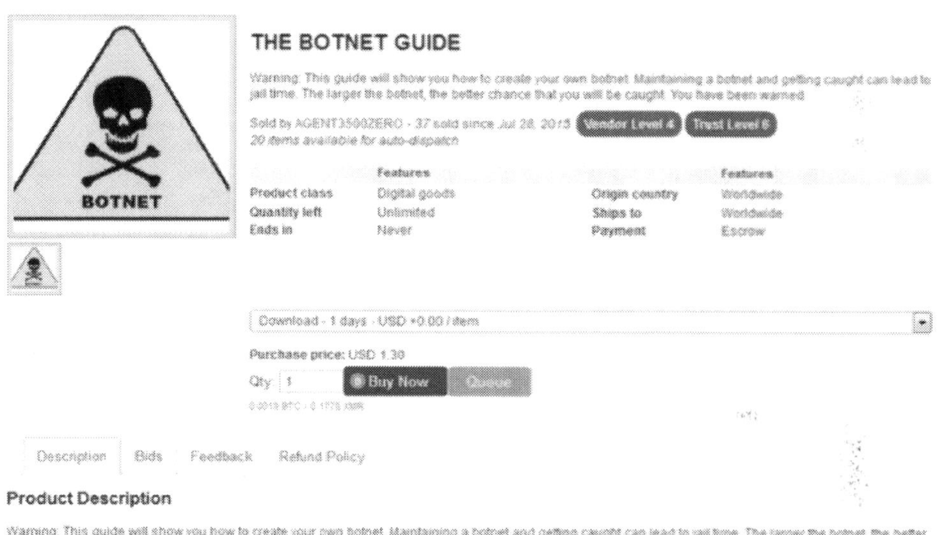

Figure 1 is of a "Botnet Guide" that is marketed to Script Kiddies on Deep Web markets such as Alphabay.

Adversaries utilize the computational resources of additional infected devices in order to amplify the magnitude of traffic that can be directed to a target system. Devices are infected with malware through watering-hole attacks, drive-by-downloads, social engineering, a buffer overflow, a 0-day exploit, or any other attack vector that enables the adversary to install the botnet malware on a machine. Some botnet malware, such as that of Zeus, Medusa, Black Energy, or Kronos, are tailored to infect specific systems when the user visits an infected site or clicks on a malicious link, such as Windows or Linux hosts. Meanwhile, other botnet malware, such as qbot, BASHLITE, and Mirai, discover and compromise clients through automated IP scanning and tools designed to brute-force access or leverage exploits against known vulnerabilities. These infected systems are known as zombies, bots, or slaves. For the purposes of this report, differences between the specific terms will be ignored. The malware on the infected system often obfuscates its presence by masquerading as a program, utility, or operating system service or it hides its presence altogether. The botnet malware may not interfere with or harm the host.

Figure 2: Deep Web Market Listing of Botnet Configuration Services

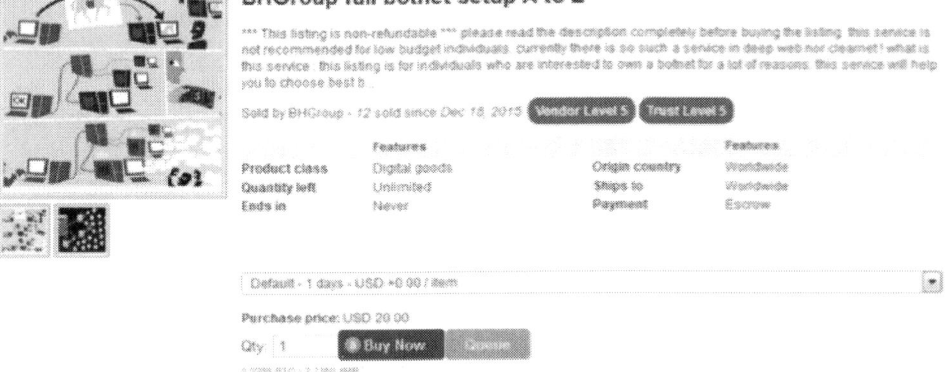

Figure 2 captures an Alphabay listing that offers to configure a botnet for a paying unsophisticated client, so that it can be used as a point and click tool.

Bots communicate with each other and with the adversary's command and control (C2) infrastructure through conventional network channels such as Internet Relay Chat (IRC) channels or peer-to-peer networking, thereby forming a botnet. Botnets are generally designed so that no single bot or group of bots acts as a single point of failure to the collective. Well- constructed botnets are highly resilient and rely on multiple channels for communication and coordination. Threat actors may use botnets to conduct DDoS attacks, to distribute malware, or as beach-heads for other attacks.

CONVENTIONAL BOTNETS

Threat actors construct conventional botnets by infecting PC hosts through malicious spam, exploit kits, infected executables, and social engineering. The bot malware provides the attacker with significant access and control of the system, but the botnets are expensive to build and operate. Purchasing a botnet usually cost approximately $0.10 per PC.

Figure 3: Deep Web Forum Posts Discussing Botnet Costs

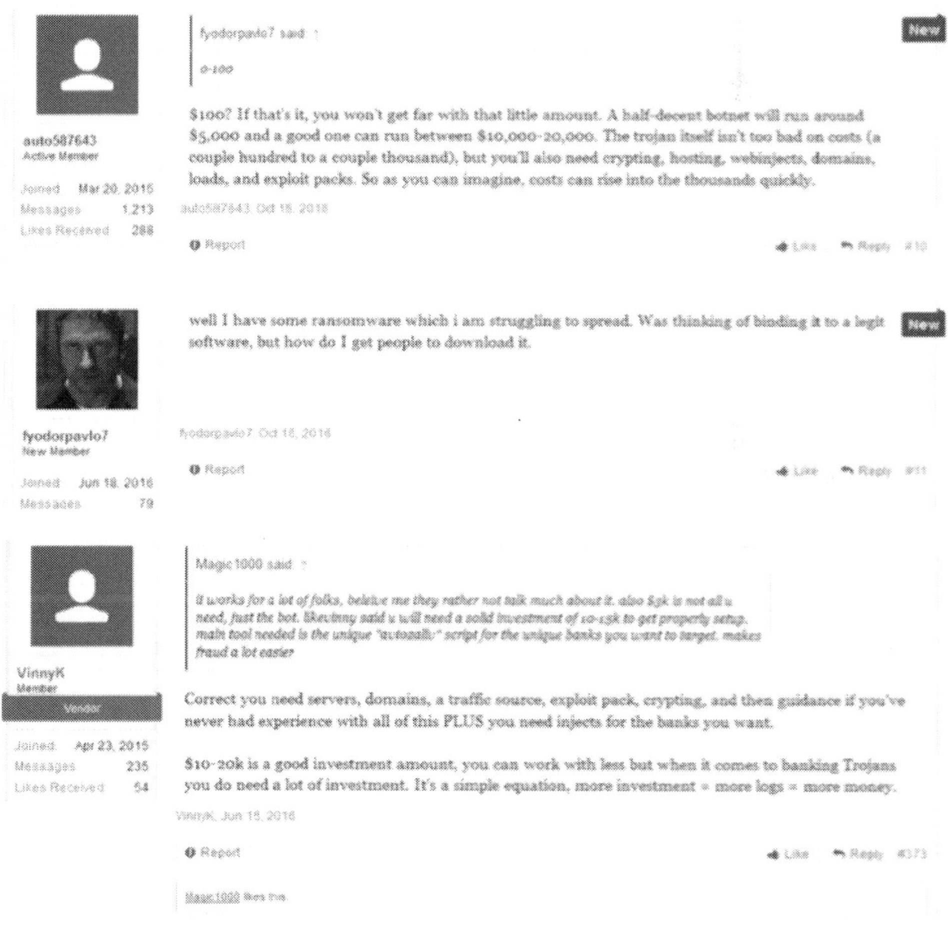

Figure 3 depicts posts from an Alphabay forum discussion concerning the cost of a botnet.

Additional time and money must be used to constantly modify the malware to avoid antivirus detection. Larger conventional botnets than Mirai have existed, but the revenue drawn from operating as a DDoS-for-hire service is insufficient compared to the overhead costs of operating and maintaining the botnet. Rather than pay ransoms to attackers, most victims can purchase an anti-DDoS service at a comparable or lesser rate. Some operators converted to "stressor" services that test the defense capabilities of a site or network. Many of these services are nothing more than a cheap Linux server running DoS scripts, operated by a script kiddie. Since the bots have dynamic IPs that change daily and since the sinkhole is often analyzed over a month, the size of reported conventional botnets is often over-exaggerated.

Conventional botnets are large and DDoS attacks are noisy enough to draw significant unwanted attention. Botnets are far more profitable when they remain unmapped and when their ability to deliver social engineering lures, RATs, ransomware, or other malware, can be capitalized.

IOT BOTNETS

IoT botnets are cheap, easy to construct, and lack significant functionality aside from DDoS attacks. As shown by Mirai, despite the declining size of the botnets, IoT botnets can deliver significant DDoS traffic and can draw proportionate attention from researchers and law enforcement. Before its debut against KrebsonSecurity, Mirai was mostly ignored because its unsophisticated telnet brute force attack was the same as that of every other IoT botnet. In a conventional botnet, only a portion of the bots are active and online at a given moment; however, IoT botnets such as Mirai, that are constructed for DDoS, are built to expand the size of the botnet and to remain actively available to the attacker. Mirai self-propagates by scanning the Internet with every bot device, though some of its bots do not have much more processing power than a pocket calculator [4]. The major downside to IoT botnets is that there is a limited pool of vulnerable target devices. Consider that a household might own five or six PCs that can be drawn into a botnet, but will likely only contain one or a few IoT devices. Further, since most of the IoT malware removes competitor scripts and blocks further exploitation, thousands of botnet operators are actively fighting for the estimated vulnerable 4000 IoT devices that become active each day.

Figure 4: Hack Forums Discussion of Mirai Saturation

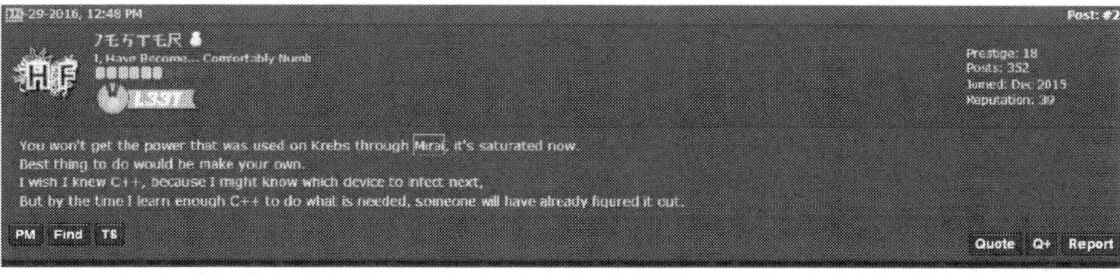

In Figure 4, a Hack Forum user opinions that Mirai is saturated.

Some script kiddies who lack the resources or the knowledge to launch attacks have begun pooling their resources to capitalize on the IoT botnet market before it dwindles to unprofitability.

Figure 5: Formation of a Script Kiddie Partnership on Hack Forums

Figure 5 captures a collaboration of Script Kiddies on Hack Forums

LAUNCHING A DDOS ATTACK

Botnets are used to launch distributed denial-of-service attacks by simultaneously directing traffic from many parallel bots against a single victim. Different bots or groups of bots can be directed to flood different targets, to flood the target with different types of traffic, to flood traffic for different intervals, or to send traffic from different sources. In this manner, some bots could launch a SYN flood, while others could launch an HTTP flood, and still others could flood a target with GRE traffic. In a reflection attack, an attacker sends a packet with a forged source IP address, apparently from the intended victim, to some server on the Internet that will reply immediately with data to the victim. This hides the source of the attack, and it can be used to overwhelm the victim with traffic from all over the world. In an amplification attack, a small forged packet elicits a large reply from the server. When combined with a reflection attack, a small amount of bandwidth coming from a small number of machines into a massive traffic load hits a victim from around the Internet. DNS, SNMP, and NTP are both popular traffic types for reflection and amplification attacks [5]. Threat actors can create layered attacks along multiple attack vectors that probe the defenses of the target, that disrupt operations, that distract a target during an attack along multiple attack vectors, or that exploit different vulnerabilities. Verisign reports that from April 1, 2016, to June 30, 2016, 64 % of DDoS attacks employed multiple attack types [3].

DDOS-AS-A-SERVICE

Many threat actors market their botnet's ability to deliver malware, spam, or floods of traffic to victims. This latter capability is referred to as a distributed denial of service attack because it aims to render distract or disrupt target operations with floods of traffic from disparate sources. The cost of a DDoS-for-hire service varies based on the size of the botnet, the type of attack, the target's defenses, the exclusivity of the malware, and other factors.

Figure 6: Alphabay DDoS-for-Hire Listing

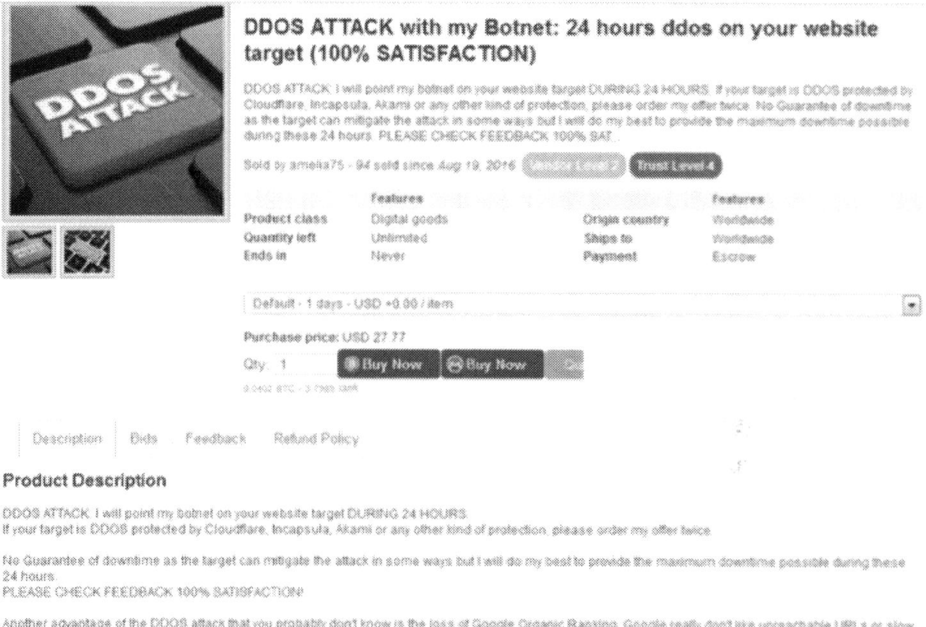

Figure 6 portrays a DDoS-as-a-service listing on the Alphabay Deep Web market.

Typical costs average between $25 and $150 per 24-hour attack against a single target. DDoS- for-hire services are marketed on Deep Web markets and forums such as Alphabay or Exploit[.]in. These services enable unsophisticated malicious users, such as average users or script kiddies, to pay to impact the operations of a target individual or organization. Worse, these for-hire services can be employed as distractions by more sophisticated adversaries as part of a layered attack.

3 | MIRAI INCIDENTS

KREBSONSECURITY

On September 20, 2016, KrebsonSecurity.com, the blog belonging to security researcher Brian Krebs, suffered a 620 Gbps DDoS attack from a Mirai and BASHLITE botnet [6]. Krebs was targeted by a DDoS-as-a-Service firm, reportedly lead by alleged Mirai author "Anna-senpai," due to his work in publicly exposing two 18-year old hackers, Itay Huri and Yarden Bidani, as the operators of the Israeli DDoS-as-a-Service, vDOS [7]. The attack was mitigated by the DDoS mitigation services provided by Akamai; however, due to the magnitude of traffic, Akamai had no choice but to "black-hole" all traffic to Krebs site into 127.0.0.1 and to disconnect Krebs site from the internet because the amount of traffic being mitigated was causing performance losses to other paying customers [6] [8]. In an interview with The Boston Globe after the attack, an Akamai official stated that it would have costed millions of dollars to continue mitigating the attack on KrebsonSecurity.com [8].

Figure 7: Script Kiddie "Anna-senpai" Hack Forums Profile

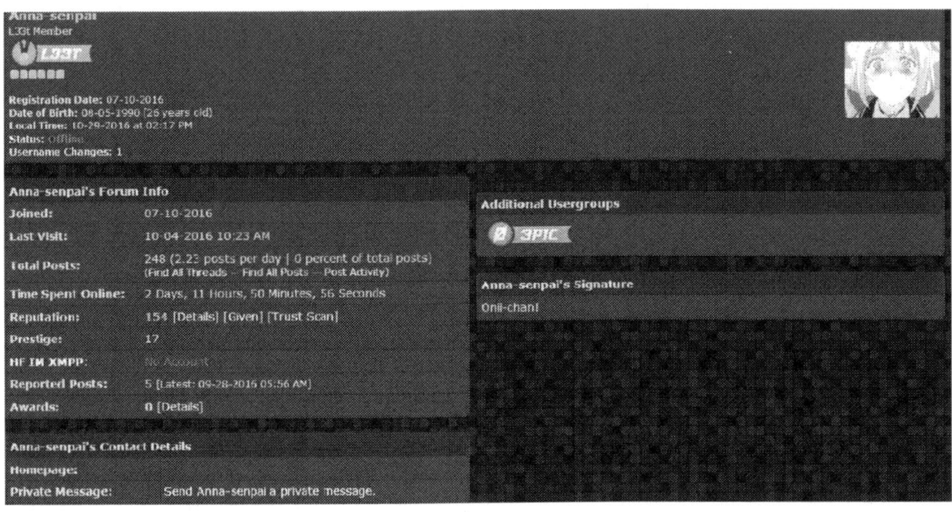

Figure 7 displays the Hack Forums profile of "Anna-senpai", the claimed author and distributor of Mirai

The botnet that targeted Krebs did not rely on amplification or reflection techniques to generate traffic; instead, it flooded his site with generic routing encapsulation (GRE) packets and with junk traffic, such as SYN, GET, and POST, which require a legitimate connection and cannot be easily spoofed. GRE is a communication protocol used to create peer-to peer networks by establishing a direct point-to-point connection between network nodes. The traffic originated from a global botnet of poorly secured IoT devices, such as routers, DVRs, and IP cameras [6].

OVH ISP

Just days after the DDoS attack on KrebsonSecurity and the exposure of the capabilities of the Mirai botnet, the French Internet Service Provider, OVH was the victim of simultaneous DDoS attacks that collected into over 1.1 Tbps of malicious traffic. The botnets involved in the attacks ranged in capabilities ranging from the ability to deliver less than 100 Gbps to the ability to deliver 799 Gbps (93MMps). IoT devices, such as DVRs, IP cameras, and routers were used in the botnets. OVH founder Octave Klaba tweeted that, "This botnet with 145607 cameras/dvr (1- 30Mbps per IP) is able to send >1.5Tbps DDoS. Type: tcp/ack, tcp/ack+psh, tcp/syn." The ISP was ultimately able to mitigate the impact of the attack and remain online; however, an attack of that magnitude of traffic would have taken offline a more strategic target such as a smaller ISP. Consider, Dyn (described below), was repeatedly taken offline with half the traffic that OVH received, and sites along the Eastern United States were momentarily unavailable [9]. No reason was given for the attack on OVH, but the script kiddie "Anna-senpai," who later released the code, claims to have lived in France at the time (though this is likely misinformation) and was avoiding law enforcement efforts in response to the attack on KrebsonSecurity.

Figure 8: Script Kiddie "Anna-senpai" Alleged Profile on Hack Forums

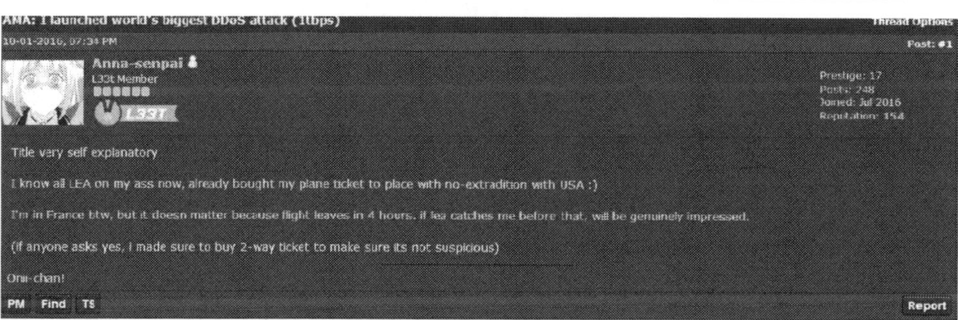

In the Hack Forum post shown in Figure 8, "Anna-senpai" claims to be pursued by law enforcement, claims to have been located in France, and he claims to have departed for a country that does not extradite to the United States. Whether any of these details are true is dubious.

ISPs are notorious for poor customer service and may therefore be common targets of disgruntled script kiddies in the future. The attack came in waves that lasted for 10 seconds, 20 minutes, and then 5 minutes and was occurred on November 16, 2016.

Figure 9: Mirai Attacks Twitter Detection of DDoS of Comcast IP Address

Mirai Attacks @MiraiAttacks · 10h

Botnet #59 - UDPPLAIN flood for 300 seconds
[Targets]
68.85.157.70/32
Port: 53

1

Mirai Attacks @MiraiAttacks · 11h

Botnet #59 - UDPPLAIN flood for 1200 seconds
[Targets]
68.85.157.70/32
Port: 53

3

Mirai Attacks @MiraiAttacks · 12h

Botnet #59 - UDPPLAIN flood for 10 seconds
[Targets]
12.122.8.83/32
Port: 53

According to Reverse-DNS, the IP address targeted in Figure 9 belongs to Comcast

More alarming is OVH's assertion that the 1.1 Tbps attack was the result of a collection of botnets because it implies that attackers are beginning to coordinate their attacks and organize in order to attempt to compromise critical infrastructure targets.

DYN

On October 21, 2016, a malicious threat actor targeted the Dyn's Managed DNS infrastructure with multiple attacks from an estimated 100,000 devices infected in a Mirai botnet that generated masked TCP and UDP traffic over port 53 [10]. External sources claim that the traffic directed at Dyn may have exceeded 1.2 Tbps. While unwilling to confirm the reported value until the conclusion of an extensive investigation, early detection of the TCP traffic at Dyn datacenters noted packet flow bursts that were 40 to 50 times greater than typical values. Further, DDoS attacks that use the DNS protocol confound the ability to distinguish between legitimate and malicious traffic. After an attack subsides, the system is further impacted by 10-20 times the amount of typical legitimate traffic from millions of IP addresses because the multiple legitimate requests had been generated from recursive servers and user attempts to access sites. The resulting traffic further exacerbates the impact of the DDoS attack.

The first attack began around 11:10 UTC in the form of elevated bandwidth against Dyn's Managed DNS platform in Asia Pacific, South America, Eastern Europe, and US-West regions. In response to the implementation of incident response protocols, the attack reconfigured to target systems relevant to the US-East region with a flood of TCP and UDP data packets from a significant number of unique IP addresses, with port 53 as the destination. In addition to their automated response, Dyn reacted to the multi-vectored attack and to the abrupt ramp-up time by employing techniques to shape incoming traffic, by manipulating anycast policies to rebalance traffic, and by applying internal filtering and scrubbing services. By 13:20 UTC, the attack subsided in response to either Dyn's mitigation efforts or in accordance with the threat actor's intent.

A second wave against Dyn's Managed DNS platform began at 15:50 UTC. The second attack incorporated a global assortment of devices and relied on the same traffic protocols, but it only lasted until 17:00

UTC because the defensive measures from the first attack remained in place and served as building points for further defense. Nevertheless, residual impacts continued until 20:30 UTC. Dyn detected smaller probing TCP attacks over the subsequent hours and days [10].

In his November 3, 2016 article for Medium.com, Security Researcher Kevin Beaumont reports that botnet #14 monitored by Malwaretech.com, belongs to the threat actor that attacked Dyn because the botnet is capable of generating malicious traffic exceeding 500 Gbps, because the botnet predates the attacks on Dyn, and because the botnet launches multiple short attacks at targets, as if it is testing their defenses.

Dyn provides essential DNS services for Twitter, Reddit, Spotify, and many other notable sites. Brian Krebs, whose blog was targeted by Mirai in late September 2016, notes that just hours before the attack, Doug Madory, a researcher for Dyn, presented a talk to the North American Network Operators Group (NANOG), based on the joint research developed with Brian Krebs, concerning duplicitous DDoS mitigation firms that act as or work with cybercriminals to launch attacks and then sell protective services to the victims. There is not conclusive data indicating that Krebs and Madory's work is the reason that Dyn was attacked; however, Krebs claims to have been contacted by a trusted source who witnessed a discussion about on a cybercrime forum about attacking Dyn, a day prior to the attack [11].

Figure 10: Script Kiddie "Anna-senpai" Admission of Guilt on Hack Forums

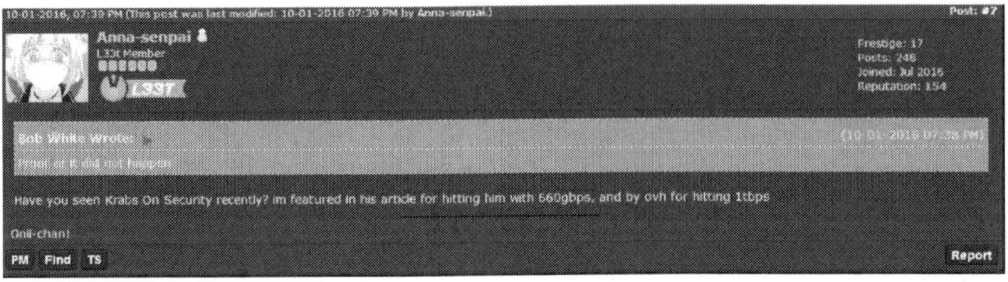

Figure 10 depicts a Hack Forums post in which "Anna-senpai" brags about conducting the Mirai attacks. It is unclear which or how many of the attacks were actually carried out by "Anna-senpai".

"Anna-senpai" claims to have attacked KrebsonSecurity.com as a DDoS-as-a-service; though, there is no conclusive attribution aside from the threat actor's forum post claiming credit and disclosing the Mirai source code. Nevertheless, if the attacks against Krebs and Dyn were retaliatory for their efforts to expose DDoS-as-a-Service operations and malicious DDoS mitigation firms, then the community will benefit from a revitalized discuss of the capabilities of less sophisticated threat actors and of how aspects of the threat landscape, such as poorly secured IoT devices, can be weaponized in devastating attacks. If the threat actor is to be believed and if the attack on Dyn was organized on cybercrime forums, then the security community may need to prepare for a massive shift in the threat landscape as less sophisticated threat actors band together to target security researchers and critical infrastructure with cutting-edge malware.

Alternately, other security researchers believe that the impact on Dyn was the result of a targeted DDoS-for-hire attack on the PlayStation Network. If true, then the attack demonstrates the vulnerability of the community as a whole, since the only major defense available to organizations are anti-DDoS services that recognize incoming attacks and redirect or redistribute the traffic to prevent downtime. If Dyn was taken offline as part of an attack on one of its clients, then with the attack adversaries have demonstrated that modern defenses are utterly insufficient to the task of preventing attacks from disrupting operations. Akamai's decision to discontinue service to KrebsonSecurity out of fears that the 620 Gbps traffic was already disrupting content delivery services to other clients, supports this conclusion. Akamai is the largest CDN, and it may operate the most servers and possess the most computational resources in the world, but it remains unclear exactly how much malicious traffic it could mitigate without falling offline in the same manner as Dyn or OVH.

Without CDNs, like Akamai, the internet would be set back to its 2006 state, and video streaming, video conferencing, real-time online gaming, and other activities that require significant bandwidth or delivered content, would no longer be available.

Regardless of the reason that Dyn suffered the attack, the incident impressed cyber-criminal communities and it justifiably inspired fearful discussions in cybersecurity and legislative communities. In his written testimony before the Congressional Committee on Energy and Commerce, Bruce Schneier stated, "In many ways, the Dyn attack was benign. Some websites went offline for a while. No one was killed. No property was destroyed. But computers have permeated our lives. The Internet now affects the world in a direct physical manner. The Internet of Things is bringing computerization and connectivity to many tens of millions of devices worldwide. We are connecting cars, drones, medical devices, and home thermostats. What was once benign is now dangerous." In the wake of the attack on Dyn, MalwareTech.com setup a Twitter account (@MiraiAttacks) that live tweets Mirai attack instructions from honeypot systems. The automated live tweets include the botnet used, the type of traffic, the duration of the attack, the target IP address, and the port targeted. At the time of publication of this report, at least 70 distinct Mirai botnets are monitored by the account and the number of adopters increases daily [12].

LIBERIA

In early November 2016, a Mirai attack against the telecommunication infrastructure of Liberia was detected in the @MiraiAttacks account. This led to speculation that an attack from a botnet based on Mirai, had taken Liberia offline [13]. One security researcher reported from anonymous sources that an attack of 500 Gbps had targeted Liberia's undersea large-transit Internet cable network and that sources confirmed intermittent internet connectivity problems in the country, corresponding to the times of the attacks. The internet cable was installed in 2011 and Beaumont alleges that it is a single point of failure for internet access [14].

This led to multiple media stories speculating that Mirai had the capability to impact the critical infrastructure of a nation state. Whether or not Mirai has the capability to disrupt a critical sector remains unknown because the claims of outages cannot be substantiated. The general manager of the Cable Consortium of Liberia reports that the African-Coast-to-Europe (ACE) submarine cable monitoring system and the servers locally hosted in the Liberia Internet Exchange Point (LIXP) show no downtime in the three weeks prior to the reports. While it is possible that a local operator experienced an outage, the Cable Consortium of Liberia did not report an incident or share relevant data with the consortium. Dyn later confirmed that routing to Liberia was stable and had been stable at the time of the alleged attack. Similarly, Akamai was unable to provide data that proved a major attack against Liberia's critical infrastructure [13]. Kpetermeni Siakor, who manages infrastructure at the Liberia Internet Exchange Point, reported that only one of the country's four major telecommunication companies, Lonestar Cell MTN, faced 500 Gbps of DDoS attack for a short period and that the attack was successfully mitigated [15].

Liberia is a small nation of 4.5 million and less than 10 percent of its population has access to the internet services offered from the nation's two providers and single shared fiber optic cable. Liberia's ACE cable also provides connectivity to at least nine other African countries and it is expected to eventually serve as many as two dozen nations in the future [16]. While this Mirai attack could have been a public demonstration of capabilities of a Mirai botnet, theories on why an adversary targeted a single carrier with a 500 Gbps Mirai attack vary. Regardless, the attack indicates that adversaries are interested in targeting information and telecommunication infrastructure for testing, extortion, or geopolitical purposes; however, since the attack was mitigated, the fractional Mirai botnets still lack the capability to wholly disrupt those sectors in even small nations [13]. The total capacity of the ACE submarine fiber-optic cable is around 5.12 Tbps [15]. At the moment, it only carries the traffic of two nations, but when it bears the traffic of 23 countries, a threat actor may be able to deny internet to numerous countries using 100,000 bots or fewer. Further, if the attacker was just testing capabilities, then other nations that rely on single points of failure or that rely on only a few network operators, may be targeted in attacks in the near future.

LAPPEENRANTA, FINLAND

From late October 2016 to November 3, 2016, a DDoS attack attributed to the Mirai botnet disrupted heating distribution to two housing blocks in Lappeenranta, Finland [17] [18]. The units were managed by a company called Valtia, a facilities services company based in Lappeenranta. The systems that controlled central heating and heated water distribution in the affected buildings failed. The systems targeted were manufactured by Fidelix, whose representative Antti Koskinen stated that vulnerabilities in the systems are opened up when operators configure the devices for convenience [17]. In an attempt to mitigate the attack, the systems automatically attempted to reboot the main control circuit and got locked in an infinite restart loop that eventually resulted in the heating system being offline for more than a week [17] [18].

The security of building automation systems is often neglected because neither managing companies nor property owners invest in network firewalls or other perimeter security. The staff that handled regular maintenance tasks were not trained to respond to network attacks [17]. Valtia identified the malfunctioning systems, switched the heating system to manual control, installed a firewall, and brought the control systems back online [18]. The firewall was configured to limit and filter the traffic to the devices [17].

According to Valtia, during the incident, "Over 90 percent of the [remote systems] in the area of terraced houses or larger buildings will not send an alarm at the moment, even if the heat is switched off or radiator pressure disappears," as the systems are designed to shut down for safety. "The systems must be actively monitored and adjusted." Media outlets are reporting the incident as a denial of service attack against the heating infrastructure of a community and attributing the attack to Mirai, in part, because the story of Finland residents stranded in the cold of winter due to a malicious DDoS attack, is an enticing story; however, the details reported might indicate a worse scenario with a less sensational story. Mirai only specifies a one hour attack time. Any attack lasting longer than an hour, launched from an original Mirai botnet, would require a threat actor to either actively redirect the bots or to write automation scripts to sustain the attack. Further, either the botnet controller or a DDoS-as-a-service client would have to possess the intent to sustain a prolonged attack against a seemingly random community. It is possible that a threat actor possessed the motivation to target the Lappeenranta community or that the attack was meant to impact a target with a similar IP range, but was sent by mistake. It is possible that the attack was the test run for some script kiddie testing out the capabilities of the botnet, probing defenses, or planning for an attack on a larger target [19].

Mirai bots scan input IP ranges for devices to compromise via brute force. It is therefore equally likely, that the automated systems controlling central heating and water for the units were themselves, IoT devices that were either infected with the DDoS malware or were subject to sustained scanning attempts that overloaded the systems and forced the reboot. Because the scanning activity to expand the botnet is automated and perpetual, the botnet or botnets overloading the heating systems with traffic would remain unaware that the heating systems were locked in a reboot cycle. If the systems were infected with the botnet malware, but lacked the computational resources to scan for other devices or execute attacks, the reboot cycle would also have been initiated. The malware or scanning activity would continue as long as the IP addresses of the devices remained active. In the former case, the botnet malware lives in the RAM of the device and would not be cleared by a flash reset. In the latter case, the scanning activity would resume on the system until all passwords in the library were attempted or until the system was compromised. It is also possible that a threat actor adapted aspects of the Mirai source code or that of another botnet to expand the attack time, to attempt additional credentials, to compromise devices along additional attack vectors, or to target new devices that the original code did not infect. The pool of devices that can be infected by the original Mirai botnet is extremely oversaturated and highly contested by the number of script kiddies and other threat actors attempting to build marketable or robust botnets. IP ranges and additional IoT devices targetable by Mirai and similar botnets can be easily discovered on Shoden and similar search engines that map the Internet. It is possible that a threat actor altered the code to infect additional IoT devices without considering whether the desired bots possessed the computational power or code base to fulfil the functions of the malware. In any case, if the devices were targeted to be drawn into the botnet rather than targeted in a DDoS attack, then the personnel could have restored the systems by simply factory resetting the devices, by changing the default credentials, by securing or disabling Telnet, and by protecting the devices behind a Firewall and other end- point security that filters and blocks traffic based on type, source, and quantity.

Any of the aforementioned scenarios in which the systems were the target of the botnet, but in which a DDoS attack was not the result of the downtime, is significantly troubling because it indicates that threat actors are expanding their presence on the IoT threat landscape by infecting new devices and adapting the malware with unknown capabilities. That the devices were not successfully incorporated into the botnet indicates that these advancements are the product of unsophisticated adversaries who are bold enough to attempt the changes and lucky enough to inflict an unanticipated impact on a number of families. If true, then even this derivative malware that bricks devices instead of incorporating them into the botnet could be adapted to cause mass panic in larger cities or to extort building owners in the same manner as ransomware, by rendering systems unavailable until payment is received.

TRUMP/ CLINTON CAMPAIGNS

Flashpoint reports that at 16:20 UTC on November 6, 2016 a 30-second HTTP Layer 7 attack targeted the campaign website of Donald Trump. 30 minutes after the attack, an actor using the username Jono Gaukster (@omegadragon97) tweeted to Donald Trump's twitter handle (@realDonaldTrump) to claim credit for the attack. Two more similar attacks targeted Trump's site at 8:13 UTC and at 8:19 UTC on November 7, 2016. In this last instance, a 30-second HTTP Layer 7 attack also targeted the site of Hillary Clinton. No outages were reported for either site. Flashpoint believes that each attack may have been carried out by a different group, who were each using the Mirai botnet [20].

The short and ultimately unsuccessful attacks suggest that unsophisticated threat actors, such as hacktivists and script kiddies, are adopting the Mirai malware and are testing it against targets who they oppose in order to cause chaos or to gain notoriety. The miniscule magnitude of generated traffic also confirms suspicions that the IoT botnet landscape has saturated with numerous threat actors who are actively competing for a limited number of IoT devices. As a result, each threat actor controls only a small IoT botnet that is not currently capable of inflicting a significant impact on a sizable target. Attackers can still leverage the botnets to gain attention, to create minor disruptions, or to distract victims while another attack vector is exploited. However, in order to launch attacks reminiscent of those against Krebs, OVH, or Dyn, attackers will need to outperform competitors or adapt the malware to compromise new varieties of IoT devices along new infection vectors [20].

On the night of November 6, 2016 and continuing for 24 hours, TCN, a phone bank service used by election campaigns, experienced a targeted DDoS attack from a Mirai botnet variant. The attack began with a small flood of junk traffic from a small pool of IP addresses, but the flow of traffic progressively increased until TCN's four 1Gbps connections to Internet providers were saturated. The adversary varied the sources and types of traffic. The most damaging traffic was DNS-amplified traffic. Even though the organization maintains ten times as much data capacity as their typical usage, the attack was able to eventually overwhelm TCN's systems.

A 4chan user using the moniker "Sparky", claimed to have launched a DDoS attack against the Clinton campaign phone lines. "Sparky" was attempting to limit the Clinton campaign's ability to connect with undecided voters on the day before the election. "Sparky" asked fellow users to "List targets here that if taken out could harm Clinton's chances of winning and I will pounce on them like a wild animal." In reality, the target, TCN, has clients on both sides of the political aisle; consequently, the attack impacted Republican campaigns as much as Democrat campaigns. The attack overwhelmed TCN's servers, periodically took its web-based software offline, and prevented volunteers and activists from accessing software that listed contacts and offered calling scripts, but it did not inhibit the phone bank's ability to make calls. TCN responded to the attack by filtering traffic, by quadrupling its number of proxy servers designed to absorb excess traffic, and by procuring anti-DDoS protection from CloudFlare to shield the organization from future attacks [21].

Despite the failure of the attack to cripple TCN operations, the DDoS did have an impact on the campaigns managed by the 80-employee firm. DDoS attacks disproportionately impact organizations like TCN, who rely heavily on volunteers because unlike paid employees, when volunteers experience frustration related to inaccessible systems, the volunteers might decide to leave or to not continue to persevere under the strain of the attack. "Sparky's" attack against TCN further demonstrated that a motivated unsophisticated adversary can attempt to target down-stream organizations in a political campaign in order to impact the results. Unlike TCN, many of these small and medium organizations lack the resources to mitigate a sustained DDoS attack.

WIKILEAKS

On November 7, 2016, the email publication servers belonging to WikiLeaks were taken offline by a targeted DDoS attack that lasted for nearly 24 hours, allegedly in response to the release "DNCLeak2", which consisted of 8263 emails allegedly stolen from the compromised account of John Podesta, chairman of the Clinton campaign [22] [23].

Regardless of opinion of WikiLeaks or the credibility of its content, the ability of an individual, collective, or nation state to suppress access to released information could have larger implications. In both the attack on WikiLeaks and the attack on KrebsonSecurity, an unknown adversary with a botnet that is small relative to the total number of targetable IoT devices, was able to disrupt the operations of a site and prevent it from conveying information. In short, DDoS attacks can be employed by malicious threat actors as cheap methods to prevent the free expression of ideas and the conveyance of information. The source code of BASHLITE, Mirai, and many other malware are publicly available online. Consequently, the ability to rapidly and cheaply obstruct any information outlet is available to any script kiddie on the internet [8].

According to estimates provided to Brian Krebs, a DDoS mitigation service capable of preventing a Mirai attack, such as the 620 Gbps attack against his blog, would cost between $150,000 and $200,000 annually. The cost of services such as these are obviously outside the reach of many individuals and small and medium businesses. Consequently, in the future, as adversaries adapt Mirai and develop more sophisticated DDoS tools that can generate more traffic more efficiently, small information outlets such as blogs, startups, and others, may be at risk of adversarial censorship [8].

At the very least, for the low cost of renting a botnet, an anonymous actor can gain the ability to prevent a whistleblower from releasing information or to stop news outlets from disseminating a story.

While this capability could be employed to limit the spread of false information, every botnet operator, every paying client, and every victim will have different opinions on what information the public deserves to access. DDoS services have always been able to silence the free expression of ideas and the conveyance of information; however, the widespread ubiquity of botnets like Mirai, the increasing capabilities of said botnets, and the decreasing sophistication necessary to build and operate powerful botnets, may indicate a future in which what information is publicly available and freely expressed is no longer the decision of information sources or readers, but is instead decided by adversaries who can easily manipulate information channels to profit from control over the flow, or lack of flow, of information on the Internet.

RUSSIAN BANKS

Figure 11: "vimproducts" Alphabay Small-Medium Mirai IoT DDoS Listing

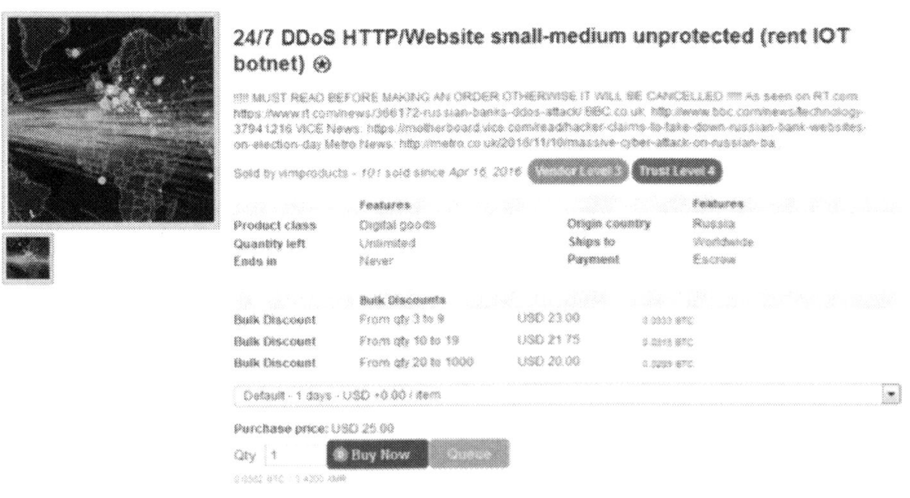

Figure 11 depicts an Alphabay listing for a DDoS-for-hire service against small-medium targets. The seller, "vimproducts," claims to have conducted the Mirai

DDoS attacks against 5 Russian banks in November 2016, on behalf of a client, in retaliation for alleged Russian involvement in the 2016 United States Presidential election.

In October 2015, eight Russian financial institutions were targeted in a DDoS campaign that inflicted a significant impact on the economy. From November 8, 2016 through November 10, 2016, at least five Russian banks, including Sberbank, Alfa-bank, the Moscow Exchange, the Bank of Moscow, and Rosbank, experienced prolonged DDoS attacks lasting from one to twelve hours, from as many as 24,000 infected IoT devices located in 30 countries [24] [25] [26]. The banks publicly claimed that the attacks did not result in any inconvenience to customers or any system downtime, though a journalist who was actively monitoring the attacked sites could not connect [25] [24]. A DDoS-for-hire service operator, "vimproducts," claimed responsibility for the attacks and alleged that a client had paid for the attacks in retaliation for Russia's alleged interference in the United States elections. The hacker directed at least one media outlet to the fully functional banking website of each target, before DDoSing it offline moments later. The actor actively sought outlets to cover the attacks in order to capitalize on the publicity. Depending on the site, the type of attack, and the security of the target, the botnet operator charges between $25 and $150 per day for an attack. Larger sites with more robust security cost more to attack. The operator also attempted to force offline the site of the Russian Ministry of Economic Development, but was unable to overwhelm its defenses [27].

Figure 12: "vimproducts" Alphabay Advanced Target IoT and PC DDoS Listing

Figure 12 depicts another, more expensive, Alphabay Mirai

4 | EVOLUTION OF IOT MALWARE

LINUX.DARLLOZ

The Linux.Darlloz was discovered in late 2013. The worm exploited an old PHP vulnerability (CVE-2012-1823) to access a system, it escalated privileges through default and common credential lists, it propagated through the network, and it established a backdoor on the system. While the original malware only infected computers running Intel x86 chip architectures, other versions were designed to target ARM, PPC, MIPS and MIPSEL chip architectures commonly used in IoT devices. The worm also scanned systems for Linux.Aidra and attempted to remove any files related to the threat and to block any ports used by Aidra for communication [28].

AIDRA

Aidra was discovered after the publication of the 2013 research paper that described the results of the 2012 Internet Census. The malware was designed to search for open telnet ports that could be accessed using known default credentials [29]. According to its author, Federico Fazzi, the malware was introduced in early 2012 as an IRC-based mass scanning and exploitation tool. The code can be compiled for MIPS, MIPSEL, ARM, PPC, x86/x86-64 and SuperH. Aidra is designed to target IoT devices that run embedded forms of Linux with active Telnet connectivity and default or no password. Some variants of Aidra can retrieve router passwords through the / cgi-bin/firmwarecfg bug found on some outdated D-Link and Netgear devices.

The malware attempts to connect to a telnet port using default credentials and if it succeeds, it downloads and executes a script called getbinaries.sh, which removes other malware binaries and prevents the device from being compromised by other competing malware. Some variants attempt to change the device credentials. Malware binaries are downloaded to /var/run, /var/tmp, /var/etc. Consequently, the malware can be removed by rebooting the device because the directories are stored in RAM. Then the infected device connects to an IRC server, joins a channel, reads a topic, and follows the instructions. Aidra is capable of scanning, flooding, and spoofing targets randomly or recursively. Further, its code can be easily tailored to a threat actor's needs [30].

QBOT/ QAKBOT

Qbot is a network-aware worm capable of harvesting credentials and creating backdoors [31]. The Qbot malware, first discovered around 2009, continues to be adapted and employed by script kiddies and cybercriminals [32]. Qbot leverages the Rig exploit kit against vulnerable websites to gain write access on the backend and to inject malicious JavaScript onto the site. To avoid suspicion, the malicious JavaScript may be appended onto the beginning or end of a legitimate JavaScript. The Rig exploit kit is a two-tier model consisting of a gate and a landing page. While a new set of domains are used for each IP address, the dense population of each IP address with many subdomains allows for a degree of undesired visibility into the botnet structure. The majority of the gate and landing page domains are registered through GoDaddy accounts; many of which are believed to be exploited compromised accounts. The Rig Gate URL returns the main_color_handle variable is returned. It contains a large string of characters that are used to determine the Rig exploit kit landing page. The string is passed through a function that replaces all illegal characters in HEX notation (0-9 and a-f) and then translates the result to ASCII and embeds the current page with an i frame with the landing page loaded with the exploit. Random variable names, dynamically generated from the Rig Gate URL contained in the kit, are used in the malicious script to obfuscate the functionality.

Users' Windows sessions are injected with the malware via a watering-hole attack or a drive-by download; alternately, modified Qbot derivatives deliver the malware through malicious emails. Once installed on the system, the malware runs a network speed test and it sends an initial beacon, containing a list of installed software, user privileges, and the infected network external IP address, to the FTP server. The malware injects itself into a running explorer.exe process and it infects processes as they start up. The bot injects a DLL into processes that will extract its strings, configuration, APIs, and critical strings block into heap-allocated buffers, when run. Qbot contains its configuration parameters, such as FTP credentials, C2 settings, and timestamps, in an internal table. The malware places system-wide inline hooks to intercept or modify network traffic, to modify or redirect browser queries, to infect new processes, and to hide its presence. Qbot uses a domain generation algorithm for all C2 communications [31].

Upon installation, modern variants contact the C2 infrastructure to receive instructions, to update, and to mutate the appearance of the malware by self-recompiling or self-re-encrypting the malware as a server-based polymorphism, an obfuscation mechanism meant to confound anti-malware application and research efforts. The server-based polymorphism enables Qbot to avoid most anti-virus products because the malware updates itself to a new version every few days, and re-encrypts itself to remain undetectable for long periods of time. The malware can detect whether it is running in a Virtual Machine sandbox and it can alter its behavior to avoid detection [32].

Once Qbot has infected a system, it begins harvesting credentials contained in Windows Credential Store (Outlook, Windows Live Messenger, Remote Desktop, Gmail Messenger) and password stored by the Internet Explorer credential manager. Further credentials are sniffed from network traffic. The attackers can use the stolen credentials and system information to access FTP servers or to infect vulnerable websites to further spread the malware [32]. Qbot attempts to spread to open shares across the network through brute force password attempts or through attempts to access the Windows Credential Store. Qbot is also capable of intercepting browser information, such as banking information, and writing the data into named pipes and then sending it to a remote server [31].

Over a two-week investigation, BAE Systems discovered over 54,517 machines infected in a Qbot botnet. Most these systems (85%) were located in the United States. The explosive popularity of Mirai and subsequent oversaturation of the IoT threat landscape has led to a decline in Qbot botnets.

Figure 13: Hack Forums Discussion of Diminishing Vulnerable IoT Device Target Pool

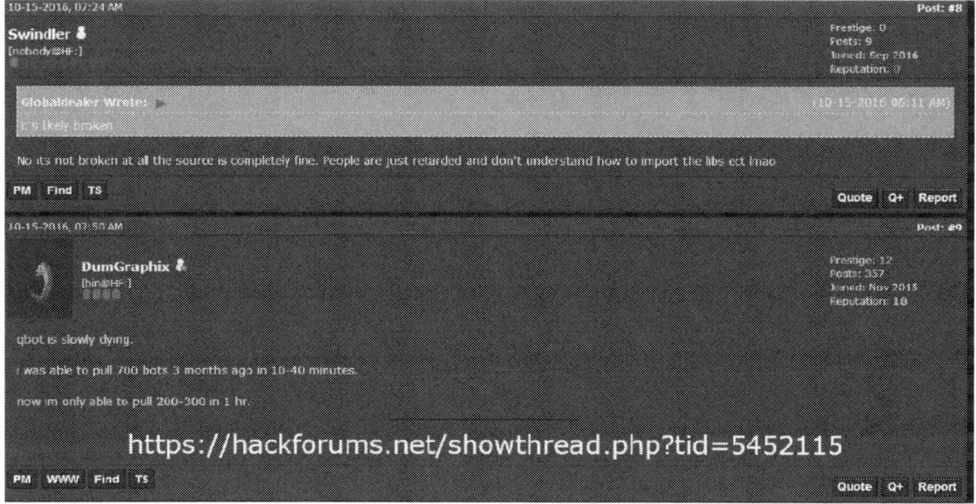

Figure 13 portrays a Hack Forums listing in which script kiddies complaining about their inability to infect IoT devices using Mirai.

BASHLITE/ LIZKEBAB/ TORLUS/ GAFGYT

BASHLITE botnets are responsible for enslaving over 1 million devices. One security firm estimates that of compromised devices, 95 percent were IP cameras or DVR units, 4 percent were home routers, and less than 1 percent were Linux servers. DVRs are high value bots because the devices are configured with open telnet and other web interfaces, often rely on default credentials, and are able to process high bandwidth, as is required to stream video. The majority of the infected devices were located in Taiwan, Brazil, and Columbia. Due to compartmentalization, the size of a monitored botnets is often difficult for security researchers to estimate. Oppositely, the C2 IPs associated with campaigns are often hardcoded into the malware and are easier to monitor [33].

The BASHLITE source code was leaked in early 2015 and has since been adapted into over a dozen variants. The malware conducts two scans to discover vulnerable devices to infect. The first attack vector utilizes the bots to port scan IP ranges for telnet servers and then it instructs them to brute force credentials in order to access and infect the device. The second attack vector employs external scanners to detect vulnerable devices and then infects those devices by using brute force on the credentials, by exploiting known security vulnerabilities, or by leveraging another attack vector [6]. Once the attacker has compromised a device, the malware tools execute the "busybox wget" and "wget" commands to retrieve the DDoS payloads. The malware does not identify the architecture of the compromised device; instead, it attempts to run different versions that have been compiled for different architectures, until one executes. Most BASHLITE attacks are simple UDP and TCP floods, though the malware does support a less used feature to spoof source addresses and some variants support HTTP attacks [33]. BASHLITE is a predecessor to Mirai, and the botnets are now in direct competition for a diminishing pool of vulnerable IoT devices [34].

MIRAI

On September 30, 2016, a script kiddie using the moniker "Anna-senpai" posted the Mirai source code on Hack Forums, in a claimed attempt to "retire" due to acquired wealth and due to a dissolving botnet base resulting from ISP intervention.

Figure 14: "Anna-senpai" Hack Forums Mirai Source Code Leak

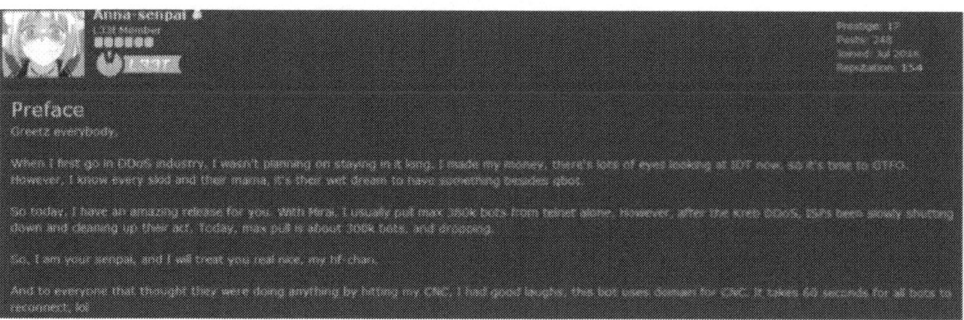

Figure 14 captures the release of the Mirai source code and instructions on Hack Forums by "Anna-senpai" in the wake of the attack on KrebsonSecurity

The actor included links to the code as well as a tutorial on how to configure the C2 infrastructure and the malware.

Figure 15: "Anna-senpai" Hack Forums Mirai Botnet Configuration and Compilation Instructions

Infrastructure Overview

- To establish connection to CNC, bots resolve a domain (resolv.c/resolv.h) and connect to that IP address
- Bots brute telnet using an advanced SYN scanner that is around 80x faster than the one in qbot, and uses almost 20x less resources. When finding bruted result, bot resolves another domain and reports it. This is chained to a separate server to automatically load onto devices as results come in.
- Bruted results are sent by default on port 48101. The utility called scanListen.go in tools is used to receive bruted results (I was getting around 500 bruted results per second at peak). If you build in debug mode, you should see the utitity scanListen binary appear in debug folder.

Mirai uses a spreading mechanism similar to self-rep, but what I call "real-time-load". Basically, bots brute results, send it to a server listening with scanListen utility, which sends the results to the loader. This loop (brute -> scanListen -> load -> brute) is known as real time loading.

The loader can be configured to use multiple IP address to bypass port exhaustion in linux (there are limited number of ports available, which means that there is not enough variation in tuple to get more than 65k simultaneous outbound connections - in theory, this value lot less). I would have maybe 60k - 70k simultaneous outbound connections (simultaneous loading) spread out across 5 IPs.

Configuring Bot

Bot has several configuration options that are obfuscated in (table.c/table.h). In ./mirai/bot/table.h you can find most descriptions for configuration options. However, in ./mirai/bot/table.c there are a few options you *need* to change to get working.

- TABLE_CNC_DOMAIN - Domain name of CNC to connect to - DDoS avoidance very fun with mirai, people try to hit my CNC but I update it faster than they can find new IPs, lol. Retards :)
- TABLE_CNC_PORT - Port to connect to, its set to 23 already
- TABLE_SCAN_CB_DOMAIN - When finding bruted results, this domain it is reported to
- TABLE_SCAN_CB_PORT - Port to connect to for bruted results, it is set to 48101 already.

In ./mirai/tools you will find something called enc.c - You must compile this to output things to put in the table.c file

Run this inside mirai directory

Code:
```
./build.sh debug telnet
```

You will get some errors related to cross-compilers not being there if you have not configured them. This is ok, won't affect compiling the enc tool

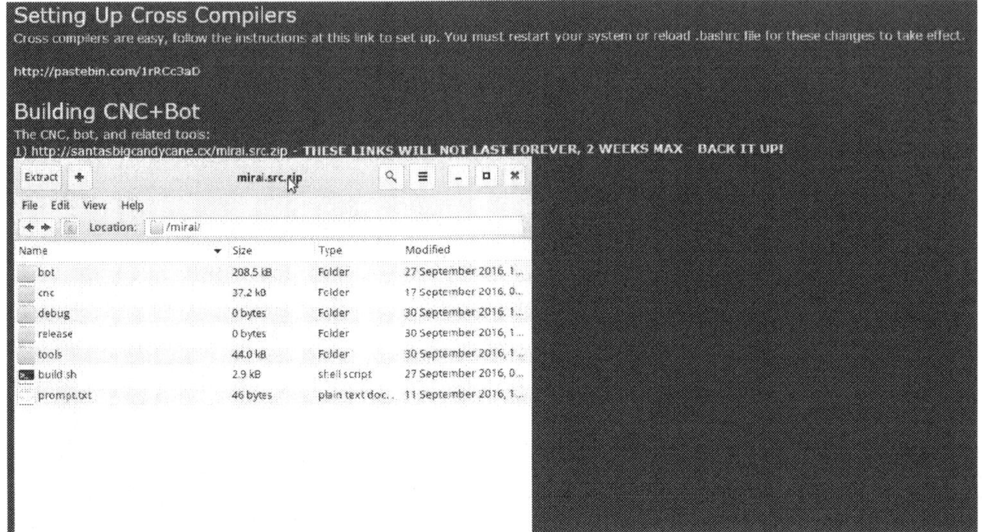

Figure 15 displays Mirai configuration and compilation instructions that follow the Hack Forums post displayed in Figure 14

The leak of the Mirai source code enabled "Anna-Senpai" to obfuscate their tracks from law enforcement, security researchers, and investigative journalists, like Brian Krebs [35].

Since the code was leaked, sporadic Mirai attacks have been detected in attacks that are believed to be new threat actors adopting the malware, exploring its functionality, and adapting its capability. Most botnets reported by security researchers consist of 40,000 – 50,000 infected devices; mostly CCTV cameras, DVRs, and home routers. Adversarial exploit of these Internet of Things (IoT) devices is not surprising [35]. Gartner estimates that by the end of 2016, the Consumer sector will harbor 4 billion IoT devices, the Cross-Industry Business Sector will rely on 1.1 billion IoT devices, and the Vertical-Specific Business Sector will operate from 1.3 billion IoT devices, for a total of 6.4 billion devices worldwide. The number of IoT devices is expected to increase to over 50 billion by 2020. The security firm, BullGuard, estimates that at present, 4.6% of observed IoT devices are vulnerable to botnets such as Mirai, Qbot, or BASHLITE

[36]. The Consumer Technology Association predicts that 170 million IoT devices will be purchased in the 2016 holiday season alone because IoT devices such as smart watches, video game consoles, smart speakers such as Amazon Echo, smart home hubs, and many other devices that feature minimal if any security, are expected to be major sale items [38].

Historically, over 60% of IoT devices are consumer devices; which is troubling considering that consumers are the group least likely to consider or improve the default security of their device [37]. A ESET and National Cyber Security Alliance study of 15,527 consumers revealed that 43% of end users had not changed the default passwords on their home routers [38]. Consumer IoT devices include any internet enabled device, such as webcams, printers, routers, mobile devices, etc. There are currently a quarter of a billion CCTV cameras worldwide [35]. In many countries, including the United States, most home users who purchase television or internet access are provided with a company specific DVR or router. These IoT devices often rely on generic or default administration credentials that most end users neglect to change. Other devices have hardcoded vendor default credentials that end users cannot change.

The IP addresses of the infected devices indicate that they are located in over 164 countries, with the highest densities in Vietnam, Brazil, the United States, China, and Mexico. The strength of the attacks ranges from 200 Gbps – 1.2 Tbps. Prior to the leak of the Mirai code, attacks predominantly flooded victims with GRE IP and GRE ETH traffic; however, since the leak, floods of traffic consist of a combination of GRE and other traffic types, such as SYN and ACK, STOMP (Simple Text Oriented Message Protocol), DNS and UDP and HTTP. The majority of the aforementioned data types are used to flood traffic on the network (OSI layer 3-4). These low-volume application layer HTTP (OSI layer 7) floods have relatively low requests per second (RPS) and originate from small numbers of source IP addresses. Though more will be added as new users adopt the malware, the default user-agents used by Mirai bots are:

» Mozilla/5.0 (Windows NT 10.0; WOW64) AppleWebKit/537.36 (KHTML, like Gecko) Chrome/51.0.2704.103 Safari/537.36

» Mozilla/5.0 (Windows NT 10.0; WOW64) AppleWebKit/537.36 (KHTML, like Gecko) Chrome/52.0.2743.116 Safari/537.36

» Mozilla/5.0 (Windows NT 6.1; WOW64) AppleWebKit/537.36 (KHTML, like Gecko) Chrome/51.0.2704.103 Safari/537.36

» Mozilla/5.0 (Windows NT 6.1; WOW64) AppleWebKit/537.36 (KHTML, like Gecko) Chrome/52.0.2743.116 Safari/537.36

» Mozilla/5.0 (Macintosh; Intel Mac OS X 10_11_6) AppleWebKit/601.7.7 (KHTML, like Gecko) Version/9.1.2 Safari/601.7.7

The varying combination of traffic types and the testing of different traffic types from a small number of bots, indicates that threat actors are still testing the threat landscape and capabilities of the malware rather than launching full-scale attacks. In the near future, Mirai is likely to shape the DDoS-as-a-Service market and to set the standard of layered attacks. As a result, the observed test behavior hints that threat actors are already at the testing stage and that widespread Mirai-driven attacks will soon target individuals, businesses, and critical infrastructure [35].

MIRAI ATTACK CHAIN

Mirai was allegedly developed as a DDoS-as-a-Service platform, competing with malware such as BASHLITE and Qbot. An attacker established a persistent TOR connection to a C2 server and a reporting server. The IP address of the C2 server periodically changes to deter mapping and attribution attempts. If the C2 server is disrupted, then the botnet takes approximately one minute to reconnect to an alternative domain. Instructions issued to the botnet and communication back to the C2 infrastructure are communicated over binary protocols. An initial number of bots scan IP ranges for vulnerable hosts (Telnet, SSH, etc.), usually on port 23 and on port 2323, and perform brute force credential attacks based on a dictionary of generic and manufacturer default credential pairs. Successful compromises are communicated from the bots to the report server as one-way traffic. The report server sends loaders to the susceptible victim IPs. The loaders use the reported credentials to compromise the victim IoT devices and to download and install the Mirai malware via a large packet port 80 communication to an IP address that hosts the malware. The victim devices are now Mirai bots and are incorporated into the larger botnet to scan for more victims or to launch DDoS attacks by directing floods of GRE IP, GRE ETH, SYN and ACK, STOMP, DNS, UDP, or HTTP traffic against a target. Targets are selected by service clients who enlist the botnet operator's service in exchange for cryptocurrencies on Deep Web markets and forums. These DDoS-as-a-Service attacks are often presented as market listings for "Server Stress Tests" and similar terms. In some cases, services were ordered via an API hosted on the C2 server.

SOURCE CODE ANALYSIS

The Mirai command and control (C2) controller was written in Go (1197 lines of code) and its botnet agent was programmed in C (5732 lines of code). The malware is designed to discover and infect Internet of Things (IoT) devices for use in targeted DDoS attacks that are coordinated based on the instructions sent from remote C2 infrastructure [35]. Mirai exclusively infects Linux devices [39]. This functionality could be expanded to include Windows devices if a more sophisticated adversary adopts the code; however, the majority of the targeted devices operate Linux, and expanding the functionality may not significantly expand the pool of botnet targets. Nevertheless, as with ransomware, one or more threat actors may attempt to add the functionality, if only to combat over-saturation of the threat landscape and victim pool.

The Mirai source code contains a number of components that will be adapted and permutated in the near future. The Build script is a simple Bash script that cleans artifacts, enables compiler flags and builds debug and release binaries via Go and GCC compilers. Mirai's Build script supports compiling bot binaries for: SPC, MIPS, x86, ARM (arm, 7, and 5n), PowerPC, Motorola 6800, and SuperH (sh4). The "admin.go" component is the primary administrative management interface. Users are greeted with a Russian language prompt (translated to "I love chicken nuggets") and are then asked to provide credentials, which are validated against a MySQL DBMS through the included "database.go" component. The malware then proceeds to print statements to the authenticated user, such as "Hiding from netstat" or "Removing all traces of LD_PRELOAD"; however, based on the code, these statements are not supported by any functions and are more likely included to mock or trick naïve users. The administration panel details the current size of the botnet and accepts input for the attack parameters (duration, type, number of bots, etc.). The hash table of bots and other associated data needed to launch an attack is included in "clientList.go". The client also balances multiple requested attacks based on the reported states of the bots (ready for attack, attacking, delete/finished current attack). The actual shell command from the administrative interface, requesting an attack, is parsed and managed by "attack.go", which also formats and builds commands, parses individual targets or delimited lists, and distributes commands to "api.go". Settings in the Attack components indicate that the time a bot can be dedicated to an attack ranges from 1 second to 3600 seconds (1 hour). The API enforces rules and bound checks and sends the commands from the C2 server to individual bots. These rules include restricting the number of bots that a user (non-administrator) can utilize in an attack, checking targets against a whitelist database, and verifying the bot state. The entry point to the C2 server binary is "main.go", which listens for inbound TCP connections on port 23 (telnet) and on port 101 (API bot responses handled by "api.go"). Inbound telnet connections indicate that a newly compromised victim will be added to the botnet (clientList.go) [40].

The bot directory, written in C, contains the attack methods the C2 server sends to the botnet. According to "attack_udp.c", bots can send User Datagram Protocol traffic in attacks, such as Generic Routing Encapsulation (GRE) floods, TSource Queries (used in bandwidth reflection and amplification attacks), DNS flood via query of type A record (hostname to IP), and floods of random bytes of plain packets. Similarly, "attack_tcp.c" indicates that Transmission Control Protocol (TCP) traffic can be used in SYN floods, ACK floods, and PSH floods. Further, Mirai supports HTTP attacks through "attack_app.c", which sends GET and POST requests consisting of numerous cookies or random payload data while masquerading as the aforementioned valid user agents, so long as the connection is maintained. The bots scan available IP addresses in select ranges for vulnerable victim hosts to infect through "scanner.c". Discovered systems are subjected to a SYN port scan. If connection to a port is established, then the bot attempts to authenticate through a brute force dictionary attack of generic and device specific credentials, or by directly authenticating via telnet. If a telnet connection is achieved, then the bot enables the system's shell/sh as needed. The bot verifies its login, then reports the victim's IP address, open ports, and authentication credentials to the C2 server and to the reporting server. Loaders leverage wget or tftp to download and install the Mirai malware on the victim host and a "killer.c" script kills competing processes on the bot, such as other malware, that utilize telnet, ssh, and other access. Finally, the "main.c" script establishes a connection back to the C2 server, initiates attacks, kills processes, and scans for additional vulnerable IoT devices [40].

BUILDING A BOTNET

Mirai scans a wide range of IP addresses and attempts to gain brute force remote access to under- secured IoT devices through a dictionary attack consisting of factory default or generic credentials [35].

Table 3: Targeted Generic Credentials

User Name	Password
666666	666666
888888	888888
admin	admin
admin	password
admin	(none)
admin	admin1234
admin	smcadmin
admin	1111
admin	1111111
admin	1234
admin	12345
admin	54321
admin	123456
admin	7ujMko0admin
admin	1234
admin	pass
admin	meinsm
admin1	password
Administrator	admin
administrator	1234
guest	guest
guest	12345
guest	12345
mother	f**er [censored]
root	xc3511
root	vizxv
root	admin
root	888888
root	xmhdipc
root	default
root	juantech
root	123456
root	54321
root	(none)
root	root
root	12345
root	pass
root	1111
root	666666
root	password
root	1234
root	klv123
root	klv1234
root	Zte521
root	hi3518
root	jvbzd
root	anko
root	zlxx.
root	7ujMko0vizxv
root	7ujMko0admin
root	system
root	ikwb
root	dreambox
root	user
root	realtek
root	0
service	service
supervisor	supervisor
support	support
tech	tech
ubnt	ubnt
user	user

Table 4: Targeted Device Specific Credentials [41]		
Device	**Username**	**Password**
ACTi IP Camera	admin	123456
ANKO Products DVR	root	anko
Axis IP Camera, et. al	root	Pass
Dahua Camera	root	vizxv
Dahua DVR	root	888888
Dahua DVR	root	666666
Dahua IP Camera	root	7ujMko0vizxv
Dahua IP Camera	root	7ujMko0admin
Dahua IP Camera	666666	666666
Dreambox TV Receiver	root	dreambox
EV ZLX Two-way Speaker	root	Zlxx
Guangzhou Juan Optical	root	juantech
H.264 - Chinese DVR	root	xc3511
HiSilicon IP Camera	root	hi3518
HiSilicon IP Camera	root	klv123
HiSilicon IP Camera	root	klv1234
HiSilicon IP Camera	root	jvbzd
IPX-DDK Network Camera	root	admin
IQinVision Cameras, et. al	root	system
Mobotix Network Camera	admin	meinsm
Packet8 VOIP Phone, et. al	root	54321
Panasonic Printer	root	0
RealTek Routers	root	realtek
Samsung IP Camera	admin	1111111
Shenzhen Anran Security Camera	root	xmhdipc
SMC Routers	admin	smcadmin
Toshiba Network Camera	root	ikwb
Ubiquiti AirOS Router	ubnt	ubnt
VideoIQ	supervisor	supervisor
Vivotek IP Camera	root	<none>
Xerox printers, et. al	admin	1111
ZTE Router	root	Zte521

Mirai contains hardcoded lists of IP addresses that are exempt from its scanning activities. These devices belong to Government, law enforcement, non-profit, and corporate entities and were likely included in an attempt to avoid drawing attention from well-resourced victims; however, the magnitude and scale of the attacks subvert any attempt by the author to remain unnoticed. Further, the list does is not expansive enough to preclude the attention of DHS, the FBI, or the NSA, who investigate cybersecurity incidents related to critical infrastructure. It is possible that the list of IPs are the remnants of a removed or preliminary feature or that the threat actor had some ulterior rationale for excluding these entities [35].

Table 5: Mirai Exempt IP Addresses

Entity	IP Address
Department of Defense	6.0.0.0/7
Department of Defense	11.0.0.0/8
Department of Defense	21.0.0.0/8
Department of Defense	22.0.0.0/8
Department of Defense	26.0.0.0/8
Department of Defense	28.0.0.0/7
Department of Defense	30.0.0.0/8
Department of Defense	33.0.0.0/8
Department of Defense	55.0.0.0/8
Department of Defense	214.0.0.0/7
General Electric (GE)	3.0.0.0/8
Hewlett-Packard (HP)	15.0.0.0/7
IANA NAT reserved	100.64.0.0/10
IANA NAT reserved	169.254.0.0/16
IANA Special use	198.18.0.0/15
Internal network	10.0.0.0/8
Internal network	192.168.0.0/16
Internal network	172.16.0.0/14
Invalid address space	0.0.0.0/8
Loopback	127.0.0.0/8
Multicast	224.*.*.*+
US Postal Service	56.0.0.0/8

Mirai contains scripts to kill any other processes that use SSH, Telnet or HTTP ports and to scrap the device memory to remove competing infections or malware, such as the "Anime" malware that also compromises IoT devices. Port 48101 is used to indicate to the botnet that the victim is already infected with Mirai in order to prevent wasting scanning activity and to prevent multiple Mirai infections. These functions prevent the infected IoT devices from becoming the hosts of multiple competing malware or botnets, it prevents remote administrators from reclaiming the devices, and it is characteristic of threat actors' fight over resources and territory in the online threat landscape. These scripts incite competition into the community that may also be one of the reasons that despite "Anna-Senpai" claiming a botnet of approximately 380,000 devices, most adopters of the malware manage botnets ranging from 40,000 to 50,000 devices [35].

ATTRIBUTION

Mirai was likely developed by a skilled, but ultimately inexperienced threat actor. Portions of the code, such as Russian strings defining the "username" and "password" fields were likely copied from other malware. In line jokes and comment references to internet memes indicate that the author is young, immature, and proficient in multiple languages [35].

REMEDIATION

At present, end users cannot prevent IoT devices from being targeted by Mirai. Device owners can limit the exploitation of their device and limit attackers' ability to develop massive botnets by unplugging and factory resetting IoT devices such as CCTV cameras, routers, and DVR units. The malware resides in memory, so unplugging the device until its reserve power source drains (if it has backup power) should rid the device from infection. Once reconnected, the user has roughly two minutes (though possible more or less time, depending on the current prevalence of the malware) to change the default or generic credentials to strong and resilient complex credentials.

Otherwise, the device is likely to be re-infected with the Mirai agent. Credentials on some devices can be changed through an administration panel that is accessible through an internet browser on the same IP subnet. Other devices require a downloaded management application from the manufacturer or supplier. Users can discover steps to manage their IoT devices by running a web search on the device or by exploring the manufacturer's website. While managing these devices, users would also benefit from installing any relevant updates or firmware patches on their device. Users should also disable remote access ports, such as port 22 (SSH), port 23 (Telnet), port 80 (HTTP) and port 443 (HTTPS) [35]. Manufacturers can play a vital role in combating Mirai and similar IoT botnets by disabling unused services, such as telnet, by default and by requiring users to set complex, unique credentials upon installation [39].

LINUX/IRCTELNET

Linux/IRCTelnet was the first discovered successor to Mirai. At the time of its discovery, Linux/IRCTelnet infected an average of 700 bots per day. Hardcoded messages in the user communication interface suggest that the malware is Italian in origin [42]. Linux/IRCTelnet borrows from Aidra, BASHLITE, and Mirai and it has the same UDP and TCP flood capabilities. Much of the malware is based on the Aidra code, but is redesigned and modified with respect to the modern IoT landscape. The malware combines BASHLITE's telnet scanner with the hardcoded credential list included in Mirai source code. Like the other IoT botnets, the malware does not establish persistence and it can be removed from infected devices by rebooting the device and clearing the RAM. The malware improves upon its predecessors with its ability to attack systems running IPv6 and its ability to communicate with bots over IRC, rather than through traditional C2 infrastructure. After compromise, the malware checks the target fork and PID and then gets the device uname data. The encoded C2 data is loaded onto the system, is decoded, and then an http request is sent to the C2 infrastructure with HTTP/1.0 to get GeoIP ("GET / HTTP/1.0\nHost: 164.132.237.180\n\n"). The GeoIP strings for the BotID are reversed and the bot connects to the IRC C2 server using "d3x" if the uname is available. An IRC connection starts and the bot listens for instructions from the C2 according to the botnet protocol [42].

5 | EVOLUTION OF MIRAI

Aspects of the Mirai malware will likely be adopted to accelerate its next generation capabilities. The design of Mirai suggests that it was built as a development platform, more than as a standalone attack tool. Script kiddies are already attempting to incorporate new credential libraries, IP ranges, target devices, traffic types, and other capabilities to expand its attack potential. Developmental trends of conventional botnets are going to be applied to the evolution of Mirai. Linux/IRCTelnet already expands the communication channel to include IRC and traffic flood to target IPv6. At the moment, Mirai activity is easy to track and C2 networks are easily mapped. In the coming months, Mirai derivatives will likely feature obfuscation features to hamper security researchers' ability to monitor activity. Some variants may even feature polymorphism. Mirai might be paired with external components such as scanners (other than Shoden), credential crackers, exploit kits, etc. Mirai can already infect ARM, ARM7, MIPS, PPC, SH4, and x86 platforms. Adversaries are actively working to expand the number of infected devices. Devices in the financial, healthcare, and energy sectors might be some of the first targets, Alternately, Mirai might be adapted to target mobile phones, similar to GM bot banking malware [43].

Figure 16: Alphabay Listing of Android Botnets

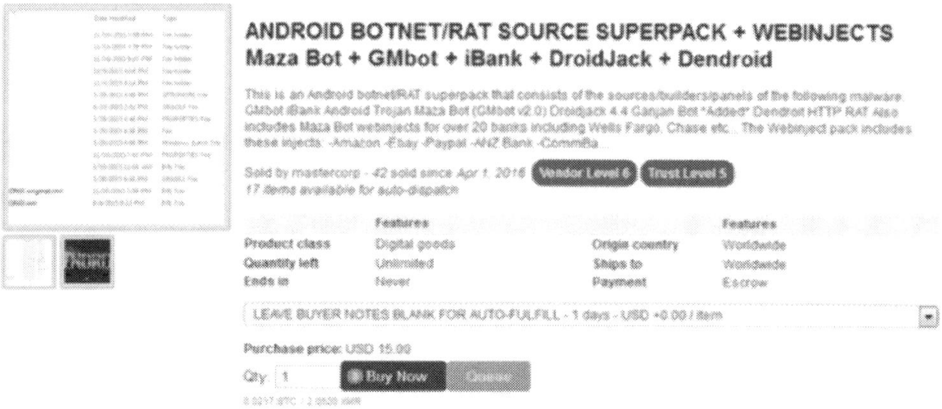

Figure 16 shows an Alphabay Deep Web listing that offers a number of Android mobile botnet malware

If a sophisticated adversary, such as an APT, takes interest in Mirai development, which is guaranteed by the magnitude and effectiveness of the attacks against Dyn and OVH, then Mirai may be evolved into a sophisticated IoT attack platform in a manner similar to Black Energy. With minor adaptions, or even the code from the worm suggested as a "solution" to Mirai, an unsophisticated adversary could adapt the code self-propagate or to "brick" or neutralize infected routers, IP cameras, DVRs, sensors, or other IoT devices. In fact, in their paper "IoT Goes Nuclear: Creating a ZigBee Chain Reaction," security researchers Eyal Ronen, Colin O'Flynn, Adi Shamir, and Achi-Or Weingarten, demonstrated that an IoT worm can be created that will infect adjacent IoT devices through networked connectivity. The researchers used the ZigBee lightbulb wireless connectivity to model an attack in which a single infected light bulb, plugged- in anywhere in a city spread within minutes so that an attacker could turn on or off all the lights in the city, "brick" all the devices, or exploit them in a massive DDoS attack [65]. If the capability to infect IoT devices with spreadable worms were built into the Mirai platform, the intact would be enormous.

The BlackNurse malware takes down enterprise firewalls with a low-volume (as little as 4 Mbps) ICMP traffic by abusing Type 3 Code 3 "port unreachable" messages, generated from a single laptop. The firewall attempts to perform stateful analysis of the packets and consumes too much computational resources. Since some filtering occurs at the perimeter, this attack could be paired with Mirai in a multi-tiered attack or some malicious actor might adapt Mirai's source code to support the attack vector [56].

On September 13, 2016, Bruce Schneier reported a pattern of DDoS activity meant to systematically stress and probe target defenses through waves of prolonged directed traffic. He postulated that the activity was the actions of a nation state sponsored APT, likely based in Russia or China, that was developing the capability to attack the global internet [44]. In 2012 a DDoS attack targeted internet root name servers. In March 2013, a group that had previously conducted DDoS attacks against Spamhaus, attacked critical Western Internet hubs such as the London Internet Exchange (LINX), the Amsterdam Internet Exchange (AMS-IX), the Frankfurt Internet Exchange (DE-CIX), and the Hong Kong Internet Exchange (HKIX). Between November 30, 2015 and December 1, 2015, a DDoS attack was launched against 13 root name servers supporting the global internet, from approximately 18,000 mobile devices that had downloaded the ISIS Android application known as Amaq Agency. In an interview with IBTimes, John McAfee claimed, "We have absolutely no defenses in place to counter this threat. If the perpetrators had activated more phones we would have lost the internet." Supposedly, when the application was running, it stored the addresses of the 13 root name servers in an encrypted packet, in memory. The addresses did not appear inside the static code for the application and the encrypted packet was only accessible while the application was active. The attacks flooded the servers with a peak of 5 million queries per second. It is estimated that as few as 18,000 devices on Wi-Fi networks could have generated that volume of traffic.

In unsophisticated attacks, Mirai managed to almost overwhelm a CDN, Akamai, and it did manage to overwhelm an ISP, OVH, and a DNS, Dyn. Targeted use of a developed Mirai derivative platform, operated by a sophisticated cyber-adversary in targeted attacks against vital Internet Critical Infrastructure, is possible and if steps are not immediately taken to mitigate the impact, the cascading outcomes could be devastating. DEFCON organizer Eddie Mize told IBTimes, "Imagine if the internet went down for several days, I believe we would see significant power grid failure and potentially loss of emergency services. This could mean the failure of dams and flood controls, power and water distribution, natural gas distribution and control failure, and more. Perhaps the most alarming aspect would be to the financial sector. I believe that loss of the internet for even a two-week period could cause enough disruption to financial institutions that consumers would lose confidence and this could be catastrophic to the markets. All of this could set up a chain reaction that could send the public in to a panicked tailspin."

6 | SECTORS AT GREATEST RISK

THE FINANCIAL SECTOR

The Financial sector is perhaps, the most consistent and constant target of distributed denial-of- service (DDoS) attacks, which heavily target financial institutions, credit card issuers, financial service suppliers, brokers and dealers, investment advisors, small financial institutions, retailers, and many other organizations. In recent years, the sector has been targeted in botnet attacks by adversaries ranging from hacktivist collectives, such as Anonymous, to cybercriminals, like Dridex, to advanced persistent threat (APT) groups, like Carbanak. For instance, from late 2011 to mid-2013, seven Iranian threat actors sponsored by Iran's Islamic Revolutionary Guard Corps launched a coordinated campaign of DDoS attacks against 46 major companies, primarily in the U.S. financial sector, over the course of 176 days. The attacks disabled victim bank websites, prevented customers from accessing web accounts, and cost tens of millions of dollars in remediation costs to neutralize and mitigate the attacks on their servers [45]. In 2013 alone, the sector sustained prolonged attacks from the hacktivist collective Anonymous, the cyberterrorist group Qassan Cyber Fighters (QCF), the Tunisian OpUSA hacktivists, and many other threat actors. Cybercriminals and hacktivists are the largest collectives, but are not the sole adversaries of the Financial sector. For instance, many of the attacks conducted by cybercriminals or cyber- mercenaries may have been contracted by nation state threat actors, cyber-jihadists, lone-wolf threats, or hail-mary threat actors, who might benefit from social panic or economic instability in the United States markets. In 2014 through 2016, many of these threat actors evolved and escalated to target the Financial sector with information stealing botnets, ransomware, and other malware instead of DDoS attacks [46].

Financial institutions are targeted with DDoS attacks that disrupt commercial processes, overwhelm communication and telecommunication networks (such as SWIFT), and degrade customer experiences by rendering financial services and web access unavailable. A botnet attack on a single financial entity can impact the entire sector or could cause a panic in the population, which results in reputational harm to financial institutions, and near-real time impacts on financial trading, market economies, and national economic stability [46] [47]. Short, intense DDoS attacks against financial institutions can cost as much as $100,000 per hour. Online banking portals, clearing interfaces, and trading applications are among the most frequent targets for DDoS. Some threat actors have begun to extort financial organizations into paying a ransom to prevent attacks against these services; as a result, some organizations have begun to stockpile Bitcoins for the express purpose of paying attackers to not attack [48]. Though paying a ransom may be cheaper than relying on an anti-DDoS service, the action does not benefit the global community. There is no guarantee that the adversary will withhold an attack or that the attacker even has the capability to launch an attack; further, as with ransomware, the payment funds cyber-terrorism, promotes cyber-hacktivism, and perpetuates the trend on profitable malicious cyber-activity in Deep Web communities.

The 2015 Verizon Data Breach Investigation Report (DBIR) found that DDoS attacks against the financial sector accounted for 32% of all cyberattacks and that 57% of financial institutions have experienced a DDoS attack [49]. In early 2016, one study found that 83% of financial services firms faced an average of 50 attempted DDoS attacks per month and required an average of 98 days to recover and initiate remediation steps. Nevertheless, only 55% of financial organizations consider DDoS a serious threat, and only 48% of organizations in the sector are confident in their ability to mitigate an attack [47].

Unlike many critical infrastructure sectors, the Financial sector has not stagnated under the threat of further attacks. Concerted efforts have focused on shifting the culture and practices to ensure that organizations understand that cyber threats and vulnerabilities are operational risk that are a shared responsibility across IT, personnel, and management. Threat information sharing is available through FS-ISAC and numerous public-private partnerships. Regulators and examiners now closely inspect institutions' risk management controls and incident response plans [46]. A 2015 Neustar study reports that as a result, 88% of banks detect DDoS attacks within 2 hours and 72% respond to the attacks within the 2-hour period [50]. The Financial sector's efforts to adapt to the evolving threat landscape is admirable, but it has not deterred threat actors. In early 2016, Anonymous launched DDoS attacks against American financial organizations as part of Operation Icarus, which they claimed targeted corrupt banks and individuals in the Financial sector [51]. Many of the script kiddies who participate in Anonymous operations are the same users who frequent forums such as Hack Forums, and are the same users currently adopting or adapting the Mirai IoT botnet code. IoT botnets will target the Financial sector in the near future, possibly as soon as the 2016 holiday season. As previously detailed, five Russian banks were already targeted by a DDoS-for-hire service operated by "vimproducts" [24].

THE HEALTHCARE SECTOR

Healthcare organizations such as insurers, pharmaceutical companies, and hospitals already suffer from cyberattacks from hacktivists, cyber-criminals, cyberterrorists, and nation state threat actors that aim to disrupt operations, extort a ransom, steal employee and patient information, or cause widespread panic. This year, ICIT's 2016 Ransomware Report recounted how medical networks were ideal targets for cybercriminals and more sophisticated adversaries. ICIT's June 2016 brief Anatomy of a Cyber-Jihad detailed how a cyberterrorist organization or a lone-wolf threat actor might target the healthcare sector in order to incite panic or as part of a multi-tiered cyber-physical attack. The brief "Your Life, Repackaged and Resold: The Deep Web Exploitation of Health Sector Breach Victims," explained how cybercriminals exchanged exfiltrated medical information on Deep Web markets and forums.

Healthcare is highly dependent on digital records, network connectivity, accessible information, and real-time communication. Obstructions to even an email server could cause delays in treatment, while widespread attacks that holistically render a critical service unavailable, such as an IoT DDoS attack, would pose a serious risk to patient and staff safety [52].

In 2014, Boston's Children's Hospital became one of the first healthcare organizations to be targeted by a cyber-hacktivist group, Anonymous, in three major strikes. Because the hospital shared an ISP with seven other healthcare organizations, the DDoS attack could have taken multiple pieces of Boston's critical healthcare infrastructure offline. On March 20, 2014, the administration of Boston Children's Hospital was notified of a Twitter message that threatened repercussions if disciplinary action was not taken against clinicians and to return a 15-year-old patient to her parents' care. The message also "doxed" or exposed the personal information, of some of the personnel targeted. In April 2104, the hospital's external website was targeted with a low-rate DDoS attack. Over the course of the following week, the attacks escalated and eventually slowed inbound and outbound traffic using TCP fragmentation floods, out-of-state floods, and DNS reflection floods (which included UDP fragment floods). Later, a third attack peaked at four times the rate of the second attack, reaching 28 Gbps [52]. The activist charged with planning the attack, Martin Gottesfeld, admitted that the attack was planned to inflict no harm on patients, but to inflict the maximum financial impact on the hospital [53]. It is important to note, that 28 Gbps is orders of magnitude less than the 620 Gbps or 1.2 Tbps generated in Mirai attacks. A Mirai attack of this scale may have taken down all eight healthcare institutions in a single attack.

On November 16, 2016, Kevin Fu, Chief Executive at Virta Laboratories testified to Congress that, "Hospitals survived not by design, but by luck. The adversary did not target healthcare. This time. Dyn represents a single point of failure for resolving Internet names, but hospitals have other kinds of single points of failure. For instance, heating and ventilation now resembles IoT with unpatched computers controlling negative pressure in units with highly infectious diseases." As discussed in ICIT's brief, "Hacking Healthcare IT in 2016: Lessons the Healthcare Industry can Learn from the OPM Breach", the Healthcare sector is incorporating, and interacting with, IoT devices that lack security-by-design. In the past, this has led to medical equipment such as MRI machines that can be infected with ransomware, morphine dispensaries that can be remotely hacked, and pacemakers that could be ransomed. The Mirai IoT target landscape is heavily saturated. While there is no indication that healthcare devices have been incorporated into DDoS botnets, it may be only a matter of time before an adversary adapt an IoT malware such as Mirai, to harness the computational resources of medical devices because many lack basic access controls such as multi-factor authentication (or any authentication whatsoever). How much would a healthcare network be willing to pay a cyber-extortionist to halt an attack that leveraged the healthcare devices within a hospital against the network? Moreover, as in the Energy sector, there is a significant danger that a more sophisticated adversary could leverage an IoT malware or a worm to "brick," or kill, infected medical devices in order to cause panic, extort a ransom, or as part of a multi-tiered attack.

THE ENERGY SECTOR

In "The Energy Sector Hacker Report: Profiling the Hacker Groups that Threaten our Nation's Energy Sector," ICIT comprehensively analyzed the threat actors and attack vectors that pose significant threat to the Energy Infrastructure of the United States. These threats included cyber- hacktivists, cyber-jihadists, cyber mercenaries, nation state threat APTs, and hail-mary threat actors. In the Energy sector, DDoS can easily impact oil and gas communication channels, electric grid networks, and other critical infrastructure assets. Consider that in a simple cyber- kinetic attack against an Oil or Natural gas rig, a DDoS attack can block most communication channels and can cheaply prevent help from reaching the personnel isolated on the platform. The sector heavily relies on IoT sensors and devices to manage the electric grid. Many, but not all, of those devices are isolated from connections external to the network; however, consider how much damage a sophisticated adversary could inflict if an IoT botnet like Mirai or one of the worms that naïve faux-experts suggest to combat Mirai, were delivered onto an Energy network and proceeded to compromise and disable IoT sensors, remote control units, and other devices.

Energy assets are high-value targets for many adversaries. International Atomic Energy Agency (IAEA) Director Yukiya Amano admitted in October 2016, that a few years ago, a nuclear power plant became the target of a targeted "disruptive cyber-attack" that was successfully mitigated [54]. Since ransomware did not popularize until early 2016, it is possible that the incident described was the result of a DDoS attack. In December 2015, the Black Energy malware was employed to systematically disable the security controls and eventually the entire Ukrainian electric grid. Black Energy began as a script kiddie/ cyber-criminal botnet, much like Mirai. With the resources and attention of a sophisticated threat actor, it was rapidly adapted into one of the most advanced malware in existence. Mirai, or IoT botnet derivatives, could easily lead to devastating attacks on the Oil and Gas industry, on the Electric grid, or on a number of Energy sector systems.

7 | RECOMMENDATIONS AND REMEDIATION

THIS IS A MARATHON, NOT A SPRINT

In the wake of the impressive Mirai DDoS attacks, a number of panicked cybersecurity professionals and faux experts have promoted rash short-term "solutions" without consideration for the long-term repercussions. One such suggestion is the employment of a controllable computer worm capable of infecting the devices vulnerable to Mirai and either removing the malware or disabling the device. Some have argued that the worm could also be used to patch, update, or actively protect devices. This solution does not consider the inevitable eventuality that a malicious threat actor will seize control of the worm or that the intended operation of the worm will have very unintended consequences. Consider how many users might be inconvenienced if their home routers and DVRs suddenly cease to function, without their consent. How might law enforcement be hindered if every one of the tens or hundreds of thousands IP cameras infected with Mirai, suddenly died? What could an adversary do with direct control of every router, IP camera, DVR, and other IoT device infected with Mirai? At the very least, how could they leverage a database that aggregated information from those devices? In short, introducing a worm or any other self-replicating or self-spreading solution to target Mirai, is just spreading more malware at the expense of the end-user.

Similarly, at least three vulnerabilities were discovered in Mirai and at least one, a stack buffer overflow, has proven capable of halting its activity. The flaw in the segment of code that conducts HTTP flood attacks can be manipulated to crash one of two forked sub-processes used in the attack; one process carries out the attack, while the other sleeps for a specified time before killing the parent process and exiting. The technique would not have prevented attacks such as those against Dyn, but it would prevent Layer 7 attack capabilities. Exploitation of the vulnerability does not prevent the attacker from reinitiating an attack, it just halts an attack in progress. However, researchers and legislators alike must be careful. Exploitation of the vulnerability to halt attacks or to otherwise hinder an adversary impacts the infected device as well and it might be illegal under the Computer Fraud and Abuse Act (CFAA), which prohibits intentional damage to a protected computer, the trafficking of passwords, intentionally damaging data on a computer, unauthorized access to government computers and data, and more. Instead of focusing the discussion on short-term solutions that might stymie Mirai attacks, cybersecurity professionals, legislators, and private sector organizations can better serve end-users by redirecting the discussion to addressing the systemic long-term problems in the IoT space and in the Internet as a whole, which enabled Mirai's success in the first place.

DEVELOP ACTIONABLE INCIDENT RESPONSE PLANS

As with all varieties of cybersecurity and cyber-hygiene, the key to an organization's survival in an increasingly hostile threat landscape is preparedness and forethought. At the moment, organizations have few technical options to mitigate DDoS aside from anti-DDoS service, endpoint security, and filtering rules. Instead, organizations can improve their security posture by developing an actionable and practiced incident response plan or standard operating procedure (SOP) for their personnel to follow in the event of an attack. These plans ensure a chain of communication and command, and they preclude rash short-term actions that could harm the organization in the long-term [46].

During the initial risk assessment and the development of an incident response plan, the information security team can harden the network against attacks by hardening configuration settings of network assets, operating systems, applications, and end-point solutions. Unnecessary services and applications should be removed from systems, and unused ports should be closed. The team can limit the likelihood of an impactful DDoS attack by implementing application and traffic whitelists, by implementing a bogon block list at the network boundary, by employing service screening on edge routers to decrease the load on stateful security devices (firewalls, etc.), by segmenting and compartmentalizing critical services, by segregating public and private services, by separating intranet, extranet, and Internet services, and by creating single-purpose servers for services such as HTTP, FTP, and DNS, where possible [46].

The plan will likely need to include information to contact the ISP, any hosting providers, and appropriate law enforcement authorities, to ensure that an incident is holistically contained and managed. Personnel will need to know whether the organization received DDoS mitigation services from an ISP or hosting provider and appropriate members of the staff will need to understand the relevant service-level-agreements (SLA). Applications and network operability will need to be tested under the DDoS mitigation service, prior to an incident because the worst time to discover that coverage is insufficient is during an attack. One aspect of this can be done by having the mitigation service generate a controlled stress traffic source of a few Gbps to validate alerting, activation and mitigation service features, and to ensure that routing and DNS remain operational under the stress of an incident. The IT or Information Security team can test small levels of traffic on the network without scrubbing and without the DDoS mitigation service in order to validate the functionality of on premise monitoring systems and to identify stress points on the network. Regular scheduled validation tests (quarterly or yearly) with the DDoS mitigation service or the Information Security team can help to ensure that the network defenses and systems are calibrated to the current threat landscape, and that the tests can ensure that network assets will not fail under DDoS attacks and can help to identify network vulnerabilities before an emerging adversary targets the network [46].

Because Mirai and other IoT botnets deliver massive floods of traffic of numerous types and from numerous sources, scenario based coverage and response plans may be the most viable options. If the attack against Dyn, which some claim was directed at the Sony PlayStation Network, is any indication, it is also in the best interests of the service provider to work with covered organizations to optimize incident response plans and DDoS mitigation controls. Organizations that outsource security services need to establish multiple communication channels with teams that manage assets such as firewalls, IDS, or the network [46].

Incident Response plans begin by identifying processes that should be followed, time-critical actions, and necessary information to acquire. After a prerequisite risk assessment, the plan will identify mission critical assets whose continued operation is essential during an incident in order to maintain resilience in the short-term and continue operations in the long-term. Essential services will be prioritized and the plan will identify what resources can be turned off or blocked during an incident in order to limit the impact of an attack and to divert as much computational resources to business continuity. Current network diagrams, IT infrastructure details, and asset inventories will help to determine actions and priorities before and during an incident. Staff and contracted services can best detect an incoming DDoS attack if the baselines of the daily network volume, types of traffic, and network performance have been regularly monitored and recorded. For instance, traffic types such as GET/POST requests can be rate limited based on IP. Analyzing the network in this manner can also identify traffic bottlenecks where a DDoS attack could prove most effective [46].

REGULATE RESPONSIBLY

On November 16, 2016, the House Energy and Commerce Committee held a hearing concerning measures to mitigate the threat of IoT botnets. A panel consisting of University of Michigan Dr. Kevin Fu, Level 3 Communications' Chief Security Officer Dale Drew and computer security researcher Bruce Schneier agreed that the manufacturers lack economic incentives sufficient to force a prioritization of security features in IoT devices [57]. Prior to the hearing, Schneier wrote on his blog that,

> "The technical reason these devices are insecure is complicated, but there is a market failure at work. The Internet of Things is bringing computerization and connectivity to many tens of millions of devices worldwide. These devices will affect every aspect of our lives, because they're things like cars, home appliances, thermostats, light bulbs, fitness trackers, medical devices, smart streetlights and sidewalk squares. Many of these devices are low-cost, designed and built offshore, then rebranded and resold. The teams building these devices don't have the security expertise we've come to expect from the major computer and smartphone manufacturers, simply because the market won't stand for the additional costs that would require. These devices don't get security

> updates like our more expensive computers, and many don't even have a way to be patched. And, unlike our computers and phones, they stay around for years and decades.
>
> An additional market failure illustrated by the Dyn attack is that neither the seller nor the buyer of those devices cares about fixing the vulnerability. The owners of those devices don't care. They wanted a webcam —- or thermostat, or refrigerator -— with nice features at a good price. Even after they were recruited into this botnet, they still work fine -— you can't even tell they were used in the attack. The sellers of those devices don't care: They've already moved on to selling newer and better models. There is no market solution because the insecurity primarily affects other people. It's a form of invisible pollution.
>
> And, like pollution, the only solution is to regulate. The government could impose minimum security standards on IoT manufacturers, forcing them to make their devices secure even though their customers don't care. They could impose liabilities on manufacturers, allowing companies like Dyn to sue them if their devices are used in DDoS attacks. The details would need to be carefully scoped, but either of these options would raise the cost of insecurity and give companies incentives to spend money making their devices secure"

The devices leveraged by the Mirai botnet, such as DVRs and routers, are not devices that users often replace. Consequently, manufacturers minimize costs and diminish the quality of the technology in hopes that users will eventually replace the device. There is little or no market incentive to patch vulnerabilities or to push updates. Nevertheless, users tend to rely on the same DVR for at least 5 years, the same router for at least 3 years, etc. [57]. Pressure to decrease production costs, to undercut competitor market prices, and to rush to market, all attribute to manufacturers' decisions to produce IoT devices that lack foundational security-by-design throughout the development cycle; in contrast, many consumers are actually willing to pay extra for devices that offer higher degrees of cybersecurity.

Manufacturers also lack regulatory oversight sufficient to alter the industry-wide norm of marginalizing security in favor of shifting the burden of risk onto the end-user. Because average end-users are not concerned about the security of tangential devices, like routers and DVR units, unless there is a catastrophic event, like the Mirai attack on Dyn, the majority of IoT devices are never secured in any way [58]. In fact, most users do not realize that devices like DVR units have configurable security interfaces.

Manufacturer negligence has made average end-users, who are unaware of the assumed burden and who are in large part ignorant of cybersecurity and cyber-hygiene best practices, complicit in the IoT botnet attacks. National IoT regulation and economic incentives that mandate security- by-design are worthwhile as best practices, but regulation development faces the challenge of balancing consumer protections and mandatory cybersecurity with manufacturer constraints in a way that promotes security-by-design without stifling innovation, and remains actionable, implementable and binding. For the sake of lasting impact instead of a market shift that avoids the regulations, national regulation seems most appropriate. State level regulation could prove asymmetric or disastrous to markets and consumers alike. Regulation on IoT devices by the United States will influence global trends and economies in the IoT space, because every stakeholder operates in the United States, works directly with United States manufacturers, or relies on the United States economy. Nonetheless, IoT regulation will have a limited impact on reducing IoT DDoS attacks as the United States government only has limited direct influence on IoT manufacturers and because the United States is not even in the top ten countries from which malicious IoT traffic originates.

A more productive discussion might focus around modern provisions to the Health Insurance Portability and Accountability Act (HIPAA), to Gramm-Leach-Billey Act (GLBA), and to other sector relevant legislation, in order to regulate the adoption and secure usage of IoT devices used in each sector as well as the security controls implemented to mitigate IoT threats. Initiatives that promote NIST 800-160 would also increase the inclusion of security-by-design as the accepted cultural norm in the IoT community [59].

BACKDOORS FOR THE "GOOD GUYS", MEANS BACKDOORS FOR THE "BAD GUYS"

Law enforcement in general, and the FBI in particular, has a reputation in the cybersecurity community for recommending initiatives and legislation that weaken native device security through weakened security controls, mandated backdoors, hardcoded administrative access, and other vectors. The vast majority of the cybersecurity community agrees that any intentional backdoor or hidden access control will be discovered by adversaries and exploited. Regardless of device, the possible harmful impact outweighs any advantage by orders of magnitude.

The Mirai IoT DDoS attacks are trivial compared to the devastation possible should a nation state or sophisticated adversary adapt the Mirai code or develop a similar capability. By weakening encryption, authentication controls, or security-by-design, the United States government would be complicit in systematically increasing the capabilities, reach, and computational resources of malicious activity. Besides, little if any actual worthwhile intelligence would be gathered from the refrigerators, routers, home thermostats, medical devices, sensors, and other IoT devices that could be burdened with hidden security bypasses.

DEVELOP PENETRATION TESTED IOT SOFTWARE AND HARDWARE FEATURING SECURITY-BY-DESIGN (NIST 800-160)

Mirai demonstrates that rapidly developed or negligently developed IoT software and hardware can and will be leveraged for malicious purposes. At this moment, every default IoT device vulnerable to Mirai and derivative botnets remains uninfected for at most three minutes due to the sheer number of cyber-adversaries vying for control of the potential bots. If IoT botnets are to be diminished and weakened in the future, IoT software and hardware must be developed with security-by-design. Device manufacturers do not include security-by-design due to lack of time, expertise, and economic incentive. While some IoT and mobile software is developed in the United States, a majority is developed or adapted abroad. Despite the possibility of regulatory measures from the United States and other nations, there is a strong likelihood that these constraints and the resulting manufacturer behaviors will remain unchanged. Rather than impose additional constraints on developers that will impact their already narrow profit margins, the cybersecurity community can build initiatives that promote the open source development and testing of IoT software.

Open source development of IoT code allows for transparent disclosure of potential vulnerabilities, it enables a community of knowledgeable cybersecurity experts to forensically test the source code for vulnerabilities and open access vectors, and it lowers the manufacturer's development costs. Some critics may argue that open source development exposes proprietary code or that it grants adversaries the same level of access afforded to security testers. Those critiques are valid and likely accurate; however, in the IoT space, openly developed code will be more valuable than proprietary developed software because it will be more resilient and more functional. In most cases, any vulnerability discovered by an attacker will be discovered, disclosed, and repaired by a security professional.

Moreover, bug bounty programs can incentivize potential adversaries to act as security testers. The development of robust, resilient open source IoT code that features security-by-design according to NIST 800-160 will have the inadvertent side effect of redirecting attackers' efforts towards compromising underdeveloped proprietary software. This additional burden may cause some widespread harm if that software is ubiquitous; however, the pressure to not suffer the reputational harm of being the "lowest hanging fruit" in the market will eventually incentivize manufacturers to incorporate security-by- design into the IoT development cycle.

IMPROVING SECURITY CONTROLS AT THE ORGANIZATION LEVEL

DDoS attacks are often distractions in multi-tiered cyberattacks, in which the threat actor seeks to weaken network defenses or to divert critical resources away from another attack vector while they establish persistent presence on the network. In other cases, botnets are used to deliver ransomware, RATs, and other malware onto network systems. Fundamental cybersecurity controls and basic cyber-hygiene training can greatly limit the number of network assets susceptible to botnet infection. This includes measures and training to ignore social engineering lures, policies enforcing hardened system authentication controls at every interface (including any open points of remote access, such as Telnet and SSH ports), defensive measures against compromised certificates, reliance on data execution prevention (DEP) and data loss prevention (DLP) services, and other essential cybersecurity controls [46].

Currently, most DDoS protection relies on proxies, load balancing, perimeter security, or an anti- DDoS service (Cloud-based or otherwise). Perimeter security is already an antiquated and inadequate defense strategy against other cyberattack vectors. Most DDoS mitigation services function by filtering traffic, redistributing traffic loads, or by redirecting floods. This strategy too, has not evolved much since the turn of the century. DDoS attacks are one of the oldest, cheapest, and easiest attack vectors. As demonstrated in the attack on KrebsonSecurity, which impacted other Akamai customers, and in the attack that took Dyn offline, which may have been focused on PlayStation Network, DDoS mitigation services from some of the largest and most resourced providers may be rapidly depreciating. Further, the continued trend of combining DDoS mitigation with DNS, CDN, and other critical infrastructure services could prove detrimental to every Internet user.

Malware such as Mirai and its inevitable derivatives demonstrate that if left un-combated, script kiddies and other unsophisticated adversaries will be able to launch or purchase severe cyberattacks against insufficiently defended targets, for little input of time, money, or technical proficiency. In proportion to the innovation occurring with DDoS malware, there is a clear market opportunity for security firms to develop bleeding-edge solutions that mitigate multi- vector DDoS threats before the attacks reach clients' security perimeters.

HOLD MANUFACTURERS ACCOUNTABLE

Mirai and other malware that infect IoT devices are designed to exploit weak security, default credentials, and hardcoded credentials and settings. Mirai utilizes a library of generic and device- specific default credentials to access and infect IoT devices. Some manufacturers, such as Panasonic, Hikvision, and Samsung have begun to require complex credentials to be created upon activation of the device; meanwhile, many others, continue to distribute devices whose default or hardcoded credentials leave the devices vulnerable to infection. In some cases, the botnets may infect devices through ports that are not secured by default or that are exposed due to Universal Plug and Play (UPnP) [41]. Some devices, such as devices made by the Chinese company XiongMai Technologies, can be accessed through a Web-based administration page (the device IP address followed by "/Login.htm), which can be bypassed without the device credentials, by navigating to "DVR.htm" prior to login [60].

Though users can clear Mirai and BASHLITE from devices by resetting devices to factory settings and changing the credentials and settings within a few minutes; some devices remain vulnerable because hardcoded settings, such as telnet or SSH credentials, remain unchanged. Moreover, activities such as changing credentials or installing the firmware and updates necessary to secure a household IoT device, are outside the attention and technical capabilities of many end users. Many home users do not know how to access devices through web interfaces to change credentials and settings, let alone how to access settings through command prompts. According to research from security firm Flashpoint, as of early October 2016, over 515,000 devices with hardcoded credentials or vulnerable hardware were actively in use by end users.

On November 16, 2016, Bruce Schneier testified to a Congressional Committee that, "We're asking consumers to shore up lousy products. It shouldn't be that there are default passwords. These devices are low profit margin, they're made offshore. And the buyer and seller don't care. I might own this DVR, you might own it. You don't know if it's secure or not. You can't test it. And you fundamentally don't care. You bought it for the features and the price." If IoT device manufacturers continue to be allowed to shift the burden on cybersecurity onto unknowledgeable consumers, then the threat posed by IoT botnets will continue to grow. While regulation may not be as viable of a control as some might hope, other solutions exist. The greatest impact on manufacturers might be achieved by realigning the burden of reputational harm with their negligent development practices. Government contractors and cooperative private sector partners have the ability to refuse to engage with manufacturers that do not incorporate security by design into devices. The media can communicate a simplification of the IoT threat to consumers, who can then make informed decisions about whether or not to purchase devices developed by manufacturers that do not practice basic cyber-hygiene or incorporate security-by-design throughout the development lifecycle.

REDUCE THE DEPENDENCE ON FOREIGN IOT DEVICES

Nearly every device vulnerable to Mirai was developed and manufactured outside the United States by manufacturers like Dahua or XiongMai. The United States is limited in its ability to regulate these manufacturers and because their products are all too often subcomponents of other imported devices, like routers or DVRs from brand name manufacturers, the ability to impose economic sanctions or restrictions is likewise limited. However, the threat posed by insecure devices is only the short-term peril of Mirai and derivative IoT malware. The design of Mirai first and foremost suggests that it was written as a development platform, more than a standalone malware. In the long-term, Mirai may be adapted by a sophisticated adversary into an advanced malware capable of inflicting devastating impacts to critical infrastructure, that make the attacks against Dyn and OVH seem trivial by comparison. Nation state activity may be the serious long- term threat of IoT malware because nearly every one of the predicted 50 billion IoT devices in active use by 2020 will have been developed and manufactured by enemy nation states.

As discussed in ICIT's legislative brief, "China's Espionage Dynasty: Economic Death by a Thousand Cuts," Chinese nation state sponsored advanced persistent threats (APTs) are directly controlled and resourced by the government. The same government has partial or majority ownership of a number of the firms that manufacture IoT devices. What few firms are not owned by the government have one or more active liaison(s) with full access to the code and systems, on site.

On November 7, 2016, the Chinese government passed its 2016 Cybersecurity Law, which among other provisions, provides the Chinese government the right to censor data, directly interact with code, and force manufacturers to purchase their equipment from a select list of providers, starting in June 2017 [61]. Further, on November 16, 2016, just hours before a Congressional panel on IoT security and hours after the White House and DHS released IoT security guidelines, a security firm released information indicating that a Chinese firm, Shanghai ADUPS Technology, that wirelessly updates software on IoT devices as well as mobile devices manufactured by ZTE, BLU, and Huawei, has been loading spyware into devices to siphon text messages, call records, and other information. The malware may allow for total control over infected devices, including the ability to remotely install or remove code without the users' knowledge. The malware cannot be detected by mobile anti-virus software because it appears as if it came installed on the device.

In a very possible that in the near-future a Chinese nation state APT, like Deep Panda or APT1, could develop an IoT malware that infected Chinese developed IoT devices through vulnerabilities or backdoor connections intentionally placed in the code, in order to monitor, disrupt, or cyber-kinetically impact American Critical Infrastructure.

PREVENT DDOS AMPLIFICATION AND REDIRECTION ATTACKS BY MANDATING BCP38

In 2000, Paul Ferguson and Daniel Senie drafted a paper on Network Ingress Filtering at the ISP level to prevent IP source address spoofing and thereby mitigate a number of DDoS attack vectors that employ amplification and reflection methods [62]. This proposed network security standard, referred to as BCP38, prevents adversaries from leveraging insecure resources (such as servers, PCs, routers, etc.) at the ISP level in DDoS attacks. In a common amplification and reflection attack, traffic is reflected from one or more third-party machines toward the intended target by sending a message to a third party, while spoofing the Internet address of the victim. When the third party replies to the message, a much larger reply is sent to the victim and the size of the attack is thereby amplified. BCP38 filters spoofed traffic before it enters the ISP network. Some providers claim to have adopted the concept of BCP38, while others refuse.

In practice, it is difficult to know which providers have or have not implemented the suggested control; but, the continued prevalence of DDoS reflection and amplification attacks indicates that a number of providers have done nothing to prevent IP spoofing despite a clear solution for over a decade [8].

The majority of the arguments against BCP38 are invalid. BCP38 drops packets that lack the IP address of the device that sent them. There are a small number of situations where packets are not fraudulent and must be manually handled by Ingress filtering. BCP38 filtering blocks packets at the very edge of the Internet, where customer links terminate in the first piece of provider 'aggregation' gear, like a router, DSLAM, or CMTS. In the early 2000s', devices that inherently featured BCP38 were cost prohibitive. Now, a majority of the carrier-grade devices in use at the ISP level already have features to implement BCP38 (even if only through access control lists (ACLs)), but the controls are not enabled because the operator lacks either the knowledge of the existence of the feature or the economic incentive to enable the feature. DDoS attacks aimed at end-users pass through ISP networks, where filtering could occur, but up until the attack on OVH, ISPs are rarely the target themselves. As such, there is little economic incentive for them to filter the traffic. Some ISPs reduce overhead by deploying old devices to filter traffic while newer devices are used for routing. In this case, the organization saves money, but the cost is transferred to end-users and is significantly increased because these devices lack BCP38 controls. Other operators are concerned with a "Tragedy of the Commons" scenario associated with training personnel and maintaining large lists of filters. In truth, information on BCP38 and filter lists are freely available online. Some believe that since ISPs offer DDoS mitigation services, they may benefit from inaction. Objectively, ISPs, to an extent, charge for bandwidth, and DDoS attacks increase the use of bandwidth, even if that cost is shifted to consumers whose devices are leveraged in the attack [63] [64]. This theory seems less likely than the simpler explanation that ISPs, like many critical infrastructure entities, are having difficulties modernizing and adapting to the ever-evolving threat landscape.

FUND AND PROMOTE INDEPENDENT CYBERSECURITY TEST-BED INITIATIVES

Kevin Fu urged Congress to consider the creation of an independent, national embedded cybersecurity testing facility modeled after the automotive crash testing conducted by the National Transportation Safety Board (NTSB). The facility could serve as a security test-bed for IoT devices, sensitive medical equipment, embedded health and safety devices, and other emerging technology. NASA's newly launched Gryphon-X program already performs a similar function by partnering with private sector organizations to develop and test bleeding-edge solutions to threats posed to critical infrastructure assets. These initiatives require funding and support proportional to the viral role that they play in protecting national cybersecurity.

CONCLUSION

The Internet has grown ubiquitous and it now permeates nearly every facet of daily life in the United States. The Internet has increased the efficiency of education, work, and innovation, but it has also increased the efficiency, ease, and viability of largescale attacks, such as the Distributed Denial-of-Service (DDoS) attacks launched from Mirai using Internet-of-Things (IoT) devices. The Mirai IoT botnet has inspired a renaissance in adversarial interest in DDoS botnet innovation based on the lack of fundamental security-by-design in the Internet and in IoT devices, and based on the lack of basic cybersecurity and cyber-hygiene best practices by Internet users. Mirai evolved from other IoT malware, such as BASHLITE, and threat actors have already begun to evolve the Mirai source code to incorporate new features and to target more devices for bot infection, in response to an oversaturation of the IoT landscape. Because the code is public, because adversaries are numerous, and because the United States has little control over IoT manufacturers, discussions in response to Mirai are better focused on the lack of security by design in the Internet and in IoT devices. Basic cybersecurity and cyber-hygiene efforts by manufacturers, legislators, and end users, can reduce the capability of botnets. Efforts at the CDN, DNS, and

ISP levels can stymie DDoS as an attack vector. If left un-combated, IoT botnets are expected to evolve in sophistication and impact for at least the next three years. Together, stakeholders can act to mitigate the impact and staunch the pervasiveness and ubiquity of IoT botnets before adversaries inflict serious impacts on critical infrastructure systems.

CONTACT INFORMATION

ICIT Contact Information:

Phone: 202-600-7250 Ext 101

E-mail: http://icitech.org/contactus/

ICIT Websites & Social Media:

www.icitech.org

https://twitter.com/ICITorg

https://www.linkedin.com/company/institute-for-critical-infrastructure-technology- icit-

https://www.facebook.com/ICITorg

SOURCES

1. "Akamai's [State of the Internet]\Security Q3 2016," in Akamai. [Online]. Available: https://www.akamai.com/us/en/multimedia/documents/state-of-the-internet/q3-2016-state-of-the- internet-security-executive-summary.pdf. Accessed: Nov. 20, 2016.

2. C. P. Pfleeger and S. L. Pfleeger, Security in computing (4th edition), 4th ed. United States: Prentice Hall PTR, 2006.

3. "Verisign Distributed Denial of Service Report Volume 3, Issue 2 - 2nd Quarter 2016," in Verisign. [Online]. Available: https://www.verisign.com/assets/report-ddos-trends-Q22016.pdf. Accessed: Nov. 13, 2016.

4. "Mapping Mirai: A Botnet case study," in MalwareTech, MalwareTech, 2016. [Online]. Available: https://www.malwaretech.com/2016/10/mapping-mirai-a-botnet-case-study.html. Accessed: Oct. 25, 2016.

5. J. Graham-Cumming, "Understanding and mitigating NTP-based DDoS attacks," in Cloudfare, Cloudflare Blog, 2014. [Online]. Available: https://blog.cloudflare.com/understanding-and-mitigating- ntp-based-ddos-attacks/. Accessed: Nov. 6, 2016.

6. B. Krebs, "KrebsOnSecurity hit with record DDoS," in KrebsonSecurity, 2016. [Online]. Available: https://krebsonsecurity.com/2016/09/krebsonsecurity-hit-with-record-ddos/. Accessed: Oct. 23, 2016.

7. B. Krebs, "Alleged vDOS Proprietors Arrested in Israel," in KrebsonSecurity, 2016. [Online]. Available: https://krebsonsecurity.com/2016/09/alleged-vdos-proprietors-arrested-in-israel/. Accessed: Oct. 23, 2016.

8. B. Krebs, "The Democratization of Censorship," in KrebsonSecurity, 2016. [Online]. Available: https://krebsonsecurity.com/2016/09/the-democratization-of-censorship/. Accessed: Oct. 23, 2016.

9. R. Millman, "OVH suffers 1.1Tbps DDoS attack," in News, SC Magazine UK, 2016. [Online]. Available: http://www.scmagazineuk.com/ovh-suffers-11tbps-ddos-attack/article/524826/. Accessed: Oct. 24, 2016.

10. S. Hilton, "Dyn analysis summary of Friday October 21 Attack," in Dyn, 2016. [Online]. Available: http://hub.dyn.com/dyn-blog/dyn-analysis-summary-of-friday-october-21-attack. Accessed: Oct. 26, 2016.

11. B. Krebs, "DDoS on Dyn impacts Twitter, Spotify, Reddit," in KrebsonSecurity, 2016. [Online]. Available: https://krebsonsecurity.com/2016/10/ddos-on-dyn-impacts-twitter-spotify-reddit/. Accessed: Oct. 23, 2016.

12. “Mirai attacks on Twitter,” in Twitter, Twitter, 2016. [Online]. Available: https://twitter.com/MiraiAttacks. Accessed: Nov. 18, 2016.

13. B. Krebs, “Did the Mirai Botnet really take Liberia Offline?,” in KrebsonSecurity, 2016. [Online]. Available: https://krebsonsecurity.com/2016/11/did-the-mirai-botnet-really-take-liberia-offline/. Accessed: Nov. 4, 2016.

14. K. Beaumont, “‘Shadows Kill’ — Mirai DDoS botnet testing large scale attacks, sending threatening messages about...,” in Medium, Medium, 2016. [Online]. Available: https://medium.com/@networksecurity/shadows-kill-mirai-ddos-botnet-testing-large-scale-attacks- sending-threatening-messages-about-6a61553d1c7#.65wgptmt6. Accessed: Nov. 6, 2016.

15. M. Kumar, “More insights on alleged DDoS attack against Liberia using Mirai Botnet,” in The Hacker News, The Hacker News, 2016. [Online]. Available: https://thehackernews.com/2016/11/ddos-attack- mirai-liberia.html. Accessed: Nov. 5, 2016.

16. L. Mathews, “Someone just used the Mirai Botnet to knock an entire country Offline,” in Forbes, Forbes, 2016. [Online]. Available: http://www.forbes.com/sites/leemathews/2016/11/03/someone-just- used-the-mirai-botnet-to-knock-an-entire-country-offline/#1bbb697351f0. Accessed: Nov. 4, 2016.

17. Janita, “DDoS Attack halts heating in Finland amidst winter,” in Metropolitan, 2016. [Online]. Available: http://metropolitan.fi/entry/ddos-attack-halts-heating-in-finland-amidst-winter. Accessed: Nov. 8, 2016.

18. M. Kumar, “DDoS Attack Takes Down Central Heating System Amidst Winter in Finland,” in The Hacker News, The Hacker News, 2016. [Online]. Available: http://thehackernews.com/2016/11/heating- system-hacked.html. Accessed: Nov. 9, 2016.

19. L. Mathews, "Hackers use DDoS Attack to Cut Heat to Apartments," in Forbes, Forbes, 2016. [Online]. Available: http://www.forbes.com/sites/leemathews/2016/11/07/ddos-attack-leaves-finnish- apartments-without-heat/#32dadd707472. Accessed: Nov. 8, 2016.

20. A. Nixon, J. Costello, and R. Tokazowski, "Flashpoint - flashpoint monitoring of Mirai shows attempted DDoS of trump and Clinton Websites," in Flashpoint Cybercrime, Flashpoint, 2016. [Online]. Available: https://www.flashpoint-intel.com/attempted-ddos-trump-and-clinton-websites/. Accessed: Nov. 7, 2016.

21. A. Greenberg, "Hackers Target Pro-Clinton Phone Banks - But Hit Trump's Too," in Wired, WIRED, 2016. [Online]. Available: https://www.wired.com/2016/11/hackers-target-pro-clinton-phone-banks-hit- trumps/. Accessed: Nov. 8, 2016.

22. A. Uzunovic, "WikiLeaks Releases DNCLeak2; Suffers Massive DDoS Attack," in HackRead, HackRead, 2016. [Online]. Available: https://www.hackread.com/wikileaks-dncleak2-suffers-massive-ddos-attack/. Accessed: Nov. 7, 2016.

23. "DDoS attack on WikiLeaks stymies new #PodestaEmails release," in RT, RT International, 2016. [Online]. Available: https://www.rt.com/usa/365845-wikileaks-ddos-attack-assange/. Accessed: Nov. 10, 2016.

24. M. Beinart, "Russia: Hackers target financial sector," in Organized Crime and Corruption Reporting Project, 2016. [Online]. Available: https://www.occrp.org/en/daily/5790-russia-hackers-target-major- russian-banks. Accessed: Nov. 14, 2016.

25. L. John, "Russian banks floored by withering DDoS attacks," in The Register, 2016. [Online]. Available: http://www.theregister.co.uk/2016/11/11/russian_banks_ddos/. Accessed: Nov. 11, 2016.

26. A. Cuthbertson, "Russian Banks Become Latest Victim of Mirai Cyberattacks," in Newsweek, Newsweek Europe, 2016. [Online]. Available: http://www.newsweek.com/russian-banks-become-latest- victim-mirai-cyberattack-botnet-520010. Accessed: Nov. 11, 2016.

27. J. Cox, "Hacker claims to take down Russian bank Websites on election day," in Motherboard, Motherboard, 2016. [Online]. Available: http://motherboard.vice.com/read/hacker-claims-to-take- down-russian-bank-websites-on-election-day. Accessed: Nov. 10, 2016.

28. "The Internet of Things: New Threats Emerge in a Connected World," in Symantec, Symantec, 2014. [Online]. Available: https://www.symantec.com/connect/blogs/internet-things-new-threats-emerge- connected-world-0. Accessed: Oct. 25, 2016.

29. M. Mimoso, C. Brook, and T. Spring, "New IoT Botnet Malware borrows from Mirai," Threatpost, 2016. [Online]. Available: https://threatpost.com/new-iot-botnet-malware-borrows-from- mirai/121705/. Accessed: Nov. 1, 2016.

30. "Lightaidra 0x2012," in House of Vierko, 2012. [Online]. Available: http://vierko.org/tech/lightaidra- 0x2012/. Accessed: Nov. 10, 2016.

31. "The Return of Qbot," in BAE Systems, 2016. [Online]. Available: https://resources.baesystems.com/pages/view.php?ref=39115&k=46713a20f9. Accessed: Oct. 26, 2016.

32. G. Cluley, "Mutating Qbot worm Infects over 54, 000 PCs at organizations worldwide," in Tripwire, Tripwire, 2016. [Online]. Available: https://www.tripwire.com/state-of-security/featured/qbot- malware/. Accessed: Oct. 26, 2016.

33. T. Spring, K. Carpenter, and M. Mimoso, "BASHLITE family of Malware Infects 1 Million IoT devices," in Threat Post, Threatpost, 2016. [Online]. Available: https://threatpost.com/bashlite-family-of- malware-infects-1-million-iot-devices/120230/. Accessed: Oct. 25, 2016.

34. B. Krebs, "Source code for IoT Botnet 'Mirai' released," in KrebsonSecurity, 2016. [Online]. Available: https://krebsonsecurity.com/2016/10/source-code-for-iot-botnet-mirai-released/. Accessed: Oct. 23, 2016.

35. I. Zeifman, D. Bekerman, and B. Herzberg, "Breaking Down Mirai: An IoT DDoS Botnet Analysis," in Imperva. [Online]. Available: https://www.incapsula.com/blog/malware-analysis-mirai-ddos- botnet.html. Accessed: Oct. 30, 2016.

36. A. Cuthbertson, "A new study shows the internet is far more vulnerable to attacks than previously thought," in News Week, Newsweek Europe, 2016. [Online]. Available: http://www.newsweek.com/internet-things-devices-cybersecurity-hackers-ddos-515437. Accessed: Nov. 6, 2016.

37. R. van der Meulen, "Gartner Says 6.4 Billion Connected 'Things' Will Be in Use in 2016, Up 30 Percent From 2015," in Gartner, 2015. [Online]. Available: http://www.gartner.com/newsroom/id/3165317. Accessed: Nov. 10, 2016.

38. L. Greenemeier, "The Internet of things is growing faster than the ability to defend it," Scientific American, 2016. [Online]. Available: https://www.scientificamerican.com/article/iot-growing-faster- than-the-ability-to-defend-it/. Accessed: Oct. 30, 2016.

39. "How the Grinch stole IoT - beyond bandwidth," in Level 3 Communications, Level 3 Communications Beyond Bandwidth, 2016. [Online]. Available: http://blog.level3.com/security/grinch- stole-iot/. Accessed: Oct. 23, 2016.

40. C. Barker, "Mirai (DDoS) source code review," in Medium, Medium, 2016. [Online]. Available: https://medium.com/@cjbarker/mirai-ddos-source-code-review-57269c4a68f#.1n4ecpxz4. Accessed: Oct. 22, 2016.

41. B. Krebs, "Who makes the IoT things under attack?," 2016. [Online]. Available: https://krebsonsecurity.com/2016/10/who-makes-the-iot-things-under-attack/. Accessed: Oct. 30, 2016.

42. A. Jain, "Meet Linux/IRCTelnet malware, the successor to Mirai!," in Cyware, Cyware, 2016. [Online]. Available: https://cyware.com/news/meet-linuxirctelnet-malware-the-successor-to-mirai- 2863deb8. Accessed: Nov. 3, 2016.

43. C. Cimpanu, "Android banking Trojans based on GM Bot infected over 200, 000 users in the past 3 months," BleepingComputer, 2016. [Online]. Available: http://www.bleepingcomputer.com/news/security/android-banking-trojans-based-on-gm-bot-infected- over-200-000-users-in-the-past-3-months/. Accessed: Nov. 7, 2016.

44. B. Schneier, "Someone is learning how to take down the Internet - Schneier on security," in Schneier on Security, 2016. [Online]. Available: https://www.schneier.com/blog/archives/2016/09/someone_is_lear.html. Accessed: Oct. 25, 2016.

45. "Manhattan U.S. Attorney announces charges against Seven Iranians for conducting coordinated campaign of Cyber attacks against U.S. Financial sector on behalf of Islamic revolutionary guard corps- sponsored entities," in United States Department of Justice, 2016. [Online]. Available: https://www.justice.gov/usao-sdny/pr/manhattan-us-attorney-announces-charges-against-seven- iranians-conducting-coordinated. Accessed: Nov. 20, 2016.

46. D. Johnson and H. Wyson, "Distributed denial of Service Attacks (DDoS)," in American Bankers Association. [Online]. Available: http://www.aba.com/tools/function/fraud/pages/distributeddenialofserviceattacks-ddos.aspx. Accessed: Nov. 12, 2016.

47. J. Brousseau, "DDoS attacks on the rise in financial sector," in Expert IP, 2016. [Online]. Available: http://blog.allstream.com/ddos-attacks-a-growing-threat/. Accessed: Nov. 7, 2016.

48. R. Prime, "How the financial sector can combat DDoS attacks," in Information Age, Information Age, 2015. [Online]. Available: http://www.information-age.com/how-financial-sector-can-combat-ddos- attacks-123460288/. Accessed: Nov. 11, 2016.

49. W. Ashford, "DDoS is most common cyber attack on financial institutions," in Computer Weekly, Computer Weekly, 2016. [Online]. Available: http://www.computerweekly.com/news/4500272230/DDoS-is-most-common-cyber-attack-on-financial- institutions. Accessed: Nov. 20, 2016.

50. P. Crosman, "Banks lose up to $100K/hour to shorter, more intense DDoS attacks," in American Banker, American Banker, 2015. [Online]. Available: http://www.americanbanker.com/news/bank- technology/banks-lose-up-to-100khour-to-shorter-more-intense-ddos-attacks-1073966-1.html. Accessed: Nov. 13, 2016.

51. S. Weagle, "Anonymous launches DDoS attacks on banks in 'op Icarus,'" in Coreor, Corero, 2016. [Online]. Available: https://www.corero.com/blog/725-anonymous-launches-ddos-attacks-on-banks-in- op-icarus.html. Accessed: Nov. 20, 2016.

52. "DDoS Case Study: DDoS Attack Mitigation Boston Children's Hospital," in Radware, 2015. [Online]. Available: https://security.radware.com/ddos-experts-insider/ert-case-studies/boston-childrens- hospital-ddos-mitigation-case-study/. Accessed: Nov. 20, 2016.

53. L. Vaas, "Anonymous hacker charged with #opJustina DDoS attacks on hospitals," in Naked Security, Naked Security, 2016. [Online]. Available: https://nakedsecurity.sophos.com/2016/10/24/anonymous- hacker-charged-with-opjustina-ddos-attacks-on-hospitals/. Accessed: Nov. 20, 2016.

54. A. Shalal, "IAEA chief: Nuclear power plant was disrupted by cyber attack," in Reuters, Reuters, 2016. [Online]. Available: http://www.reuters.com/article/us-nuclear-cyber-idUSKCN12A1OC. Accessed: Nov. 15, 2016.

55. M. Mimoso and C. Brook, "Mirai vulnerability disclosed, but exploits may constitute hacking back," in Threatpost, Threatpost, 2016. [Online]. Available: https://threatpost.com/mirai-vulnerability- disclosed-but-exploits-may-constitute-hacking-back/121644/. Accessed: Nov. 10, 2016.

56. P. Loshin, "BlackNurse hits big routers with low-volume denial-of-service attack," in Search Security, Search Security, 2016. [Online]. Available: http://searchsecurity.techtarget.com/news/450402917/BlackNurse-hits-big-routers-with-low-volume- denial-of-service-attack. Accessed: Nov. 14, 2016.

57. "Cyberattacks and the Internet of Things," in C-SPAN, 2016. [Online]. Available: https://www.c- span.org/video/?418599-1/hearing-focuses-cyberattacks-internet-things. Accessed: Nov. 18, 2016.

58. C. Bing, "After Dyn cyberattack, lawmakers seek best path forward," in Cyber Scoop, Cyberscoop, 2016. [Online]. Available: https://www.cyberscoop.com/ddos-dyn-house-commerce-and-energy-bruce- schneier/. Accessed: Nov. 16, 2016.

59. M. Khera, "Are regulations the answer to better Internet of things security?," in Cyberscoop, Cyberscoop, 2016. [Online]. Available: https://www.cyberscoop.com/iot-security-op-ed-dyn-ddos- mandeep-khara/. Accessed: Nov. 10, 2016.

60. B. Krebs, "Europe to push new security rules amid IoT mess," in KrebsonSecurity, 2016. [Online]. Available: https://krebsonsecurity.com/2016/10/europe-to-push-new-security-rules-amid-iot-mess/. Accessed: Oct. 23, 2016.

61. I. Thompson, "China passes new Cybersecurity law – you have seven months to comply if you wanna do biz in middle kingdom," in The Register, 2016. [Online]. Available: http://www.theregister.co.uk/2016/11/07/china_passes_new_cybersecurity_laws/. Accessed: Nov. 9, 2016.

62. P. Ferguson and D. Senie, "BCP 38 - network Ingress filtering: Defeating denial of service attacks which employ IP source address Spoofing," 2000. [Online]. Available: https://tools.ietf.org/html/bcp38. Accessed: Nov. 15, 2016.

63. "BCP38," 2016. [Online]. Available: http://www.bcp38.info/index.php/Main_Page. Accessed: Nov. 15, 2016.

64. A. McConachie, "Anti-Spoofing, BCP 38, and the tragedy of the commons," in Internet Society, Deploy360 Programme, 2014. [Online]. Available: http://www.internetsociety.org/deploy360/blog/2014/07/anti-spoofing-bcp-38-and-the-tragedy-of-the-commons/. Accessed: Nov. 20, 2016.

65. E. Ronen, C. O'Flynn, and A.-O. Weingarten, "IoT goes nuclear - creating a ZigBee chain reaction,". [Online]. Available: http://iotworm.eyalro.net/. Accessed: Nov. 18, 2016.

Made in the USA
Columbia, SC
25 May 2017